John Hedgecoe's Guide to Photography

Mitchell Beazley

John Hedgecoe's Pocket Guide to Practical Photography
was edited and designed by
Mitchell Beazley International Ltd
Michelin House, 81 Fulham Road, London SW3 6RB

Contents

Contents (continued)

Equipment/Choosing a camera

Camera designs today offer a wide variety of picture sizes, viewfinders and body shapes and styles. Before you buy a camera find out which type is best suited to your requirements and what its capabilities are (see pp. 6-10).

A camera can be categorized by the size of negative it takes, the film type or size, or its viewing method. All cameras can be divided into two main groups—reflex and non-reflex; this refers to the viewing system. A reflex camera provides the photographer with an image of the subject as seen on a ground-glass viewing/focusing screen reflected by either a fixed mirror, in the case of the twin lens reflex (TLR), or a flip-up mirror, in the case of the single lens reflex (SLR). Also in this group are the roll-film cameras, which take either 120 or 220 film for larger negatives. Format sizes are 6 x 4.5 cm ($2\frac{1}{4}$ x $1\frac{3}{4}$ in), 6 x 6 cm ($2\frac{1}{4}$ x $2\frac{1}{4}$ in) and 6 x 7 cm ($2\frac{1}{4}$ x $2\frac{3}{4}$ in). Some of the 6 x 6 cm cameras are TLRs and some are SLRs, some of the SLRs have optional attachments for alternative format sizes.

Non-reflex cameras have direct-vision viewfinders and include the following formats: sub-miniature, 110, 126, 35 mm and half-frame 35 mm (these names refer to the film size they take).

In addition there are the view cameras (also called technical or studio cameras and used mainly by professionals) and several models of instant-picture cameras.

 35 mm SLRs These may be manually operated or automatic; they have a wide variety of accessories and an enormous selection of lenses. With a manual model both aperture and shutter speed must be adjusted for the correct exposure. An automatic is either shutter-priority or aperture-priority: with the former you set the required shutter speed and the camera selects the correct aperture; with the latter you set the required aperture and the camera selects the correct shutter speed. There are two models that will work in both ways and also have a full manual override control.

35 mm non-reflexes These have the advantage of a reasonable negative size, but the disadvantage of not accepting interchangeable lenses; however, screw-in close-up (or supplementary) lenses may be used for close-ups. They suffer from parallax error (see p. 6). Many of these cameras have automatic exposure systems.

 110 and disc Compact and inexpensive, these cameras are ideal for informal photography where a larger camera might be an encumbrance. Their main disadvantage is the small negative size, which limits quality.

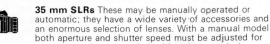 **Medium-format reflexes** Medium-format SLR cameras enjoy a growing popularity at the expense of the TLR. The SLR uses roll-film with negative sizes of 6 x 4.5 cm ($2\frac{1}{4}$ x $1\frac{3}{4}$ in), giving 15 shots per roll of 120 film; 6 x 6 cm ($2\frac{1}{4}$ x $2\frac{1}{4}$ in), which is the most common format and provides 12 shots per film; and 6 x 7 cm ($2\frac{1}{4}$ x $2\frac{3}{4}$ in), giving 10 shots. Medium-format SLRs accept a range of interchangeable lenses. However, the choice for the TLR is very limited and the lenses are expensive. A further problem associated with the TLR is parallax error.

 Instant-picture cameras Instant-picture cameras give you a fully developed single print immediately. Their disadvantages are their bulky size (though they are not heavy) and lack of negatives. Accessories are usually limited.

35mm SLR

The 35 mm single lens reflex is the most sophisticated and versatile of cameras. Continual improvement in both film and lens performance has ensured that the 35 mm format, once disparaged as being too small for good-quality enlargement, is now completely acceptable to amateur and professional photographers alike. The modern SLR usually forms part of a camera system embracing a wide choice of lenses, flash equipment, and other accessories.

A reflex mirror set at 45° in the pentaprism—the camera's central hump—conveys to the viewfinder exactly what the lens sees. When you press the shutter release, the mirror swings up in advance of the shutter's opening, allowing light from the subject to pass through the lens and fall on the film, so that an image is recorded. After exposure, the mirror returns to its original position. The shutter is of the focal plane design in which two metal blinds move in rapid sequence across the film during exposure. The length of the exposure is determined by the size of the gap between the blinds. Most SLRs offer a maximum shutter speed of 1/1000 or 1/2000 second.

All modern SLRs have an integral light meter that helps you select the right exposure or, increasingly, sets exposure completely automatically. Most models also offer a range of automatic functions besides exposure control, the most important being electronic focusing, or autofocus.

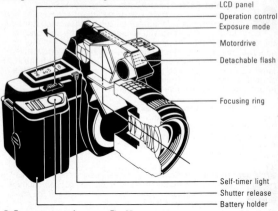

- LCD panel
- Operation control
- Exposure mode
- Motordrive
- Detachable flash
- Focusing ring
- Self-timer light
- Shutter release
- Battery holder

▶ **Exposure control systems** The 35 mm SLR uses a light-sensitive cell to measure the intensity of light coming through the lens ("TTL"). TTL metering at its most basic allows you to select manually both the aperture and shutter speed to obtain correct exposure. With an aperture-priority model (like the one shown, right) you select the aperture setting and the camera sets the corresponding shutter speed. The procedure is reversed with shutter-priority models. Fully automatic cameras combine aperture and shutter-speed settings according to the light. Multimode cameras offer the choice of manual, priority, or fully automatic ("program") modes.

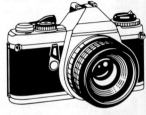

Medium-format SLR

The medium-format or roll-film SLR is a highly dependable camera favoured by professionals and adopted by an increasing number of keen amateurs. The 120 film it uses produces an image that is, typically, four times larger than that of the 35 mm SLR, making for high quality. The most common type has a negative size of 6 × 6 cm (2¼ × 2¼ in), giving 12 exposures per roll of film. The other formats are 6 × 4.5 cm (2¼ × 1¾ in) and 6 × 7 (2¼ × 2¾ in), which give 15 and 10 exposures respectively with 120 film.

The viewing system incorporates, like its 35 mm counterpart, a 45° mirror, but the image is reflected on to a horizontal viewfinder that is looked into at waist rather than eye level. Since there is no pentaprism to correct the orientation of the image, it is seen as reversed left to right. Pentaprisms are available, however, for some models. Medium-format SLRs accept a range of interchangeable lenses and, unlike 35 mm models, are designed for use with film backs. These are interchangeable light-tight magazines which allow you to change part of the way through a film from, for example, colour to black and white or even instant-picture film.

These cameras are normally used with a hand-held light meter, for critical metering, but with some models a metering device can be fitted over the focusing screen. Exposure selection is sometimes automatic, but focusing is always manually controlled.

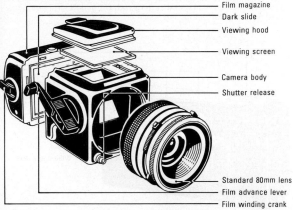

- Film magazine
- Dark slide
- Viewing hood
- Viewing screen
- Camera body
- Shutter release
- Standard 80mm lens
- Film advance lever
- Film winding crank

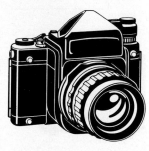

▶ The 6 × 7 cm camera Sometimes known as the "ideal format", the 6 × 7 cm (2¼ × 2¾ in) image allows for minimal wastage of the negative area. The Pentax 6 × 7 camera resembles a scaled-up 35 mm SLR, offering a pentaprism as standard and having a shape and arrangement of controls similar to those of the smaller camera. When the camera is used on a tripod, the mirror can be locked up to reduce vibration. Some other 6 × 7 models feature a revolving film back that makes for ease of transition between horizontal and vertical framing. These cameras are especially suitable for action photography, where quick responses are required.

35mm compact

Non-reflex cameras of this type have long been known as direct vision cameras because the viewing system is separate from the lens. However, advances in microcircuitry have allowed these cameras to become progressively smaller, so that they are now characterized chiefly by their compactness. The principal drawback of the compact camera is that the lens cannot be exchanged for others of different focal length, which limits the treatment of any subject to the view obtained through a standard (50 mm) or, in some cases, 35 mm lens. The exception is the model with a zoom lens (see below).

A few models still use the rangefinder focusing system in which two viewing lenses measure the focusing distance by comparing two separate images. When these images are aligned, by means of the focusing ring on the lens, the subject is in focus However, autofocus has become practically a standard feature of the sophisticated automation offered by the latest compacts. Similarly, exposure control is automatic in most models, so that all you have to do is point the camera and shoot. Some models confirm that exposure is correct or, when there is insufficient light, use the built-in flash that most cameras now have. As with SLRs, a degree of manual control is available: the viewfinder displays the aperture or shutter-speed setting that you have selected, while the camera's light meter allows it to make the complementary setting for correct exposure. Other automatic features include film-speed setting with DX-coded film, and film loading, transport, stop, and rewind.

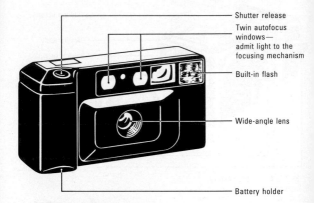

Shutter release

Twin autofocus windows— admit light to the focusing mechanism

Built-in flash

Wide-angle lens

Battery holder

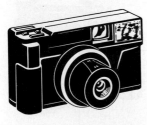

◖ **The zoom compact** has an adjustable, non-detachable lens which can be set to any focal length within a limited range, automatically changing the size of the image in the viewfinder. There are also some models that offer a choice of two different focal lengths. Typically, zoom compacts are highly automated, with high-accuracy autofocus. The example shown has a range of 35–70 mm.

Instant-picture camera

Instant-picture cameras provide a fully developed print within about two minutes of exposure. Most cameras have automatic exposure control with a slight lighten/darken adjustment possible. Some accessories are available, but choice is very limited. Film tends to be expensive. The advantage is being able to see a print straight away: the disadvantage is that once the picture is taken, you can get a second identical print only by specially copying the first. The exception is Polaroid film Type 665, which yields a black and white print and a reusable negative. Most have direct vision viewfinders and some have fixed-focus lenses. Some models have direct vision and rangefinder focusing, but SLR viewing and autofocus are now widely available.

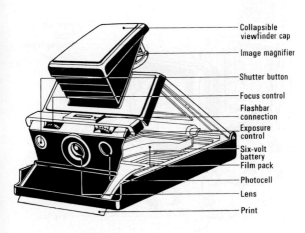

- Collapsible viewfinder cap
- Image magnifier
- Shutter button
- Focus control
- Flashbar connection
- Exposure control
- Six-volt battery
- Film pack
- Photocell
- Lens
- Print

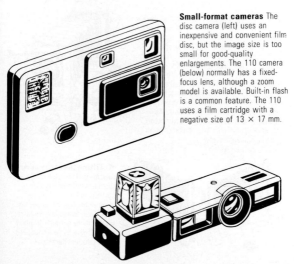

Small-format cameras The disc camera (left) uses an inexpensive and convenient film disc, but the image size is too small for good-quality enlargements. The 110 camera (below) normally has a fixed-focus lens, although a zoom model is available. Built-in flash is a common feature. The 110 uses a film cartridge with a negative size of 13 × 17 mm.

9

View camera

View cameras are simple in design, yet extremely versatile. They use sheet film measuring typically 10.2 x 12.7 cm (4 x 5 in), which is suitable for large-scale, specialist photography such as landscapes and architecture. The monorail type shown here (the most common design today) must be mounted on a tripod during use.

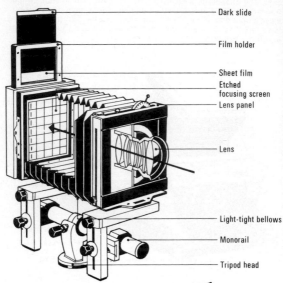

Dark slide

Film holder

Sheet film

Etched focusing screen

Lens panel

Lens

Light-tight bellows

Monorail

Tripod head

▶ **View cameras** can be adjusted while the image is viewed on the focusing screen. They have a variety of adjustments besides the usual ones for focus, aperture and (leaf) shutter speed, but they are not usually all found on a single camera. The back and front may each be made to rise, fall, slide, tilt, swing and revolve either separately or in various combinations to achieve the desired view of the subject. All these movements are with respect to the lens and film axes. After final adjustments, the focusing screen is replaced by the film holder. The film may be of the instant-picture type, or it may be in sheets or rolls.

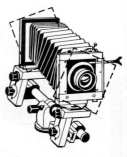

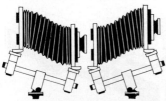

◀ **Tilting the entire camera** upwards will bring the whole of tall structures into the lens's view, but vertical lines will appear to converge. Correct perspective is achieved by keeping the camera level with the ground (film plane perpendicular to the ground) and raising the lens panel.

Lenses

Most cameras employ complex lenses, so light of different wavelength (and hence different colour) entering any part of the lens can be brought into focus at the film plane. An iris diaphragm built into the lens allows the aperture to be varied (settings are called f stops). A common range for a standard lens is between f2.8 (widest) and f16 (smallest). Apertures are varied to control exposure and depth of field (the area of sharpness around the point of true focus).

Lenses come in a variety of focal lengths. For a 35 mm format camera a 50 mm lens is standard, but for a 6 × 6 cm (2¼ × 2¼ in) format an 80 mm lens is needed to fill the larger negative area with the same image. For the 35 mm format, a 135 mm telephoto lens gives a bigger image of a distant scene than a 28 mm wide-angle; a wide-angle has a greater field of view (in this case, 74° as opposed to only 18°).

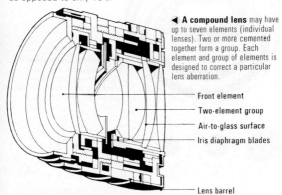

◄ **A compound lens** may have up to seven elements (individual lenses). Two or more cemented together form a group. Each element and group of elements is designed to correct a particular lens aberration.

Front element

Two-element group

Air-to-glass surface

Iris diaphragm blades

Lens barrel

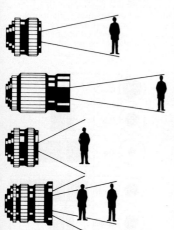

◄ **A normal (or standard) lens** gives an image size that approximates the view as seen by the human eye. Most fixed-lens cameras have a standard lens.

◄ **A telephoto lens** has a narrow angle of view (sometimes only 2°), but produces an image large enough to fill the negative so the subject appears larger

◄ **A wide-angle lens** fills the negative with up to 180° of the scene by reducing subject size. This is an advantage when shooting large groups or in a restricted area.

◗ **Zoom lenses** allow you to select any focal length in a range between two fixed points. The most popular are moderate wide-angle to standard (28–50 mm) and short-to-medium telephoto (80–200 mm). Zooms with "shortest to longest" ratios greater than 1:3 are often inferior.

Lenses

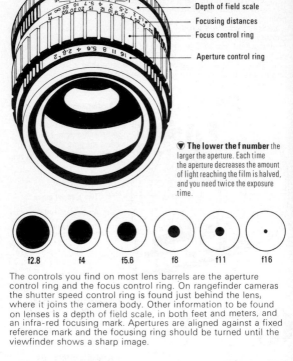

Focus reference mark
Depth of field scale
Focusing distances
Focus control ring
Aperture control ring

▼ **The lower the f number** the larger the aperture. Each time the aperture decreases the amount of light reaching the film is halved, and you need twice the exposure time.

| f2.8 | f4 | f5.6 | f8 | f11 | f16 |

The controls you find on most lens barrels are the aperture control ring and the focus control ring. On rangefinder cameras the shutter speed control ring is found just behind the lens, where it joins the camera body. Other information to be found on lenses is a depth of field scale, in both feet and meters, and an infra-red focusing mark. Apertures are aligned against a fixed reference mark and the focusing ring should be turned until the viewfinder shows a sharp image.

▶ **Changing aperture** affects both exposure and depth of field. The smaller the aperture the greater the depth of field; more of the area behind and in front of the subject will be rendered acceptably sharp. The effect of opening up one stop (f11 instead of f16) doubles the amount of light entering the lens and, to maintain correct exposure, the exposure time needs to be halved (1/125 instead of 1/60).

▶ **Changing focal length** affects not only image size but also depth of field. A 135mm telephoto lens gives a greater image size than does a 28 mm wide-angle lens, but the depth of field associated with a lens at a given aperture and focusing distance is also affected by focal length. Assuming a consistent aperture and focusing distance, the shorter the focal length the greater the depth of field.

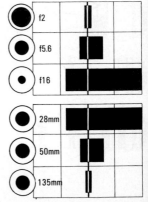

f2
f5.6
f16

28mm
50mm
135mm

The greater a lens's focal length the less its angle of view. As the focal length increases the minimum focusing distance also increases. The minimum focusing distance for a 50 mm lens may be 0.45 m ($\frac{1}{2}$ yd), but the closest object a 250 mm telephoto lens can focus on may be as distant as 6 m ($6\frac{1}{2}$ yd).

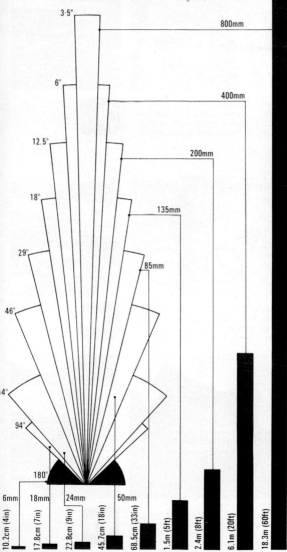

Lenses

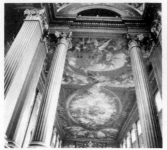
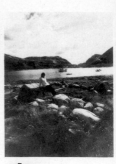

15 mm Ultra wide-angle for interiors—it embraces a wide view without undue distortion—and for landscapes it can take in the immediate foreground and the sky almost directly overhead.

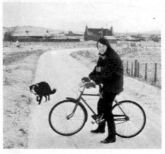
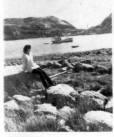

28 mm The wide-angle I prefer. It has an extensive depth of field and produces virtually no distortion. Notice how images diminish or increase according to the lens you use.

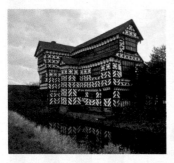
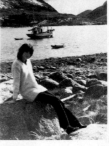

50 mm Closest to human eyesight, this lens gives a "normal" relationship between different image planes. It has the fastest apertures and is the ideal general-purpose lens.

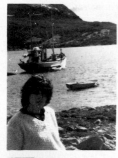

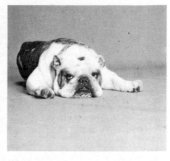

135 mm The longest easily hand-held lens; ideal for portraiture. It pulls the background up sharply, enabling you to get close-ups of difficult subjects from a reasonable distance.

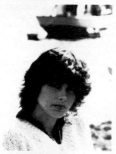

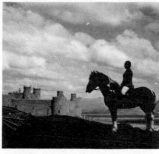

200 mm Excellent for close-ups and useful for relating middle-distance subjects and background. If you want to hand hold you must shoot at 1/250 or more. *f*4 is usually the widest aperture available.

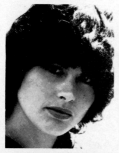

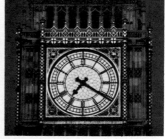

Tele-converter This enables you to extend the focal length; a 2x converter turns a 200 mm into a 400 mm, as above. There is a slight loss in definition, but results are acceptable.

Black and white filters

Filters are simply pieces of coloured transparent material (usually glass) that screw into the threaded mount on the front of your lens. They work on the principle of allowing some light components to pass through the filter and reach the film while blocking others. For example, a blue filter will let blue light pass through and block yellow, orange and red. In this way shades of grey produced by a black and white film can be manipulated either to resemble the tonal strengths of a scene as viewed by the eye more closely, or to emphasize parts of a scene that would normally pass unnoticed because of the film's inability to reproduce all colours as different shades of grey.

You do not need a large range of filters for black and white photography. Limit yourself to only two or three to start with— a yellow filter to darken skies slightly and make foliage appear lighter; an orange filter to accentuate the contrast between sky and cloud and bring out the texture of such surfaces as brick and wood, and a UV or haze filter, which is a general-purpose filter used for eliminating the worst effects of ultraviolet light, pronounced in distant scenes or near large expanses of water. (For further details see p.132.)

Care of filters is vital. Before attaching a filter make sure it is free from dust and fingerprints. If dirty, clean with a soft, lint-free cloth or lens tissue. Greasy or scratched filters will seriously degrade the images produced by the finest optics. Lens-cleaning fluid can also be used to remove particularly stubborn marks. Always replace the filter in its case when it is not in use.

Each photograph on the page opposite was taken using a different filter. The picture below is unfiltered to act as a comparison. All pictures were shot on HP5 using a Pentax with 35 mm lens. Exposure was varied each time to compensate for the light-blocking strength of each filter. (For details on filter factors, see table on p.132.)

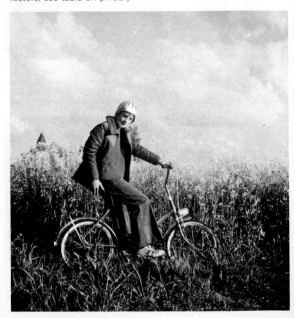

▶ **A yellow filter** was used, right, to lighten the foreground and middle-distance vegetation. This is a useful filter to have if you plan to do a certain amount of landscape photography as it also has the effect of increasing the contrast between cloud and sky slightly.

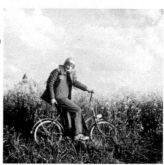

▶ **The green filter** right, has darkened the boy's jumper quite considerably. His trousers, which are blue, now appear slightly darker and tonal contrast in the sky has become slightly stronger.

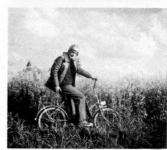

▶ **Using a blue filter** has noticeably altered the atmosphere of the photograph, right. Instead of a bright sunny day the weather now appears very misty. Contrast between sky and cloud has completely disappeared and the cyclist's trousers now seem almost white. Shadow detail has also decreased.

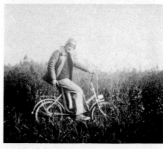

▶ **A red filter** produces the most pronounced sky effects. The clouds in this shot are now clearly distinguishable from the background sky. The blue of the cyclist's trousers now appears darker than in the unfiltered shot and his jumper is now white. This filter needed the greatest exposure allowance—three stops.

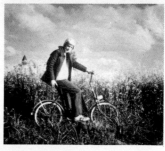

Light meters

If your camera does not have a built-in light meter and you find it difficult judging exposures by using the recommended camera settings accompanying the film pack, the best way to guarantee accurate exposure is to use a hand-held meter. These meters give you a range of alternative shutter speeds and aperture settings, and are preferred by many professionals.

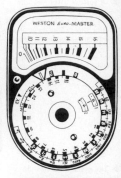

▶ **The selenium cell exposure meter** needs no outside power source. When exposed to light the cell generates an electrical current in direct proportion to the amount of light falling upon it. This, in turn, activates a needle, which moves across a calibrated scale indicating various shutter speeds and aperture combinations. In bright light the selenium cell is as accurate as most other light meters, but in low light conditions a flap that normally covers the cell must be removed.

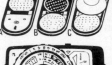

▶ **CdS (cadmium sulphide) cell exposure meters** have a wide sensitivity range and are reliable in low light, but they do tend to "remember" a high light reading for a short time after exposure. The CdS meter, although very similar in appearance to the selenium cell meter, needs a small battery to activate it. The cell becomes a resistor, restricting an electrical current in proportion to the light reaching it.

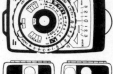

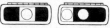

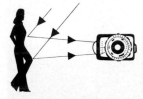

▲ **A reflected light reading is** adequate for most situations—especially landscapes and medium-toned subjects. The light meter cell is pointed at the subject and measures the light reflected back. All TTL meters work on this principle.

▲ **An incident light reading is** a measure of the light falling on the subject. A diffuser cone, to enlarge the angle of acceptance of the light-sensitive cell, is placed over the cell, which is then pointed back towards the light source.

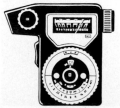

◀ **A spot meter** is basically a light meter that measures reflected light only, and cannot be used for an incident reading. As its name implies, it has a very narrow angle of light acceptance—in some cases as little as 1°—as opposed to about 40° with a normal light meter. The spot meter is designed to be used with subjects that cannot be approached, and has a window that allows a direct view of the subject for accurate sighting.

▶ **Built-in light meters** are a feature of most modern cameras. Rangefinder cameras usually have the cell positioned to one side of the front element of the lens or near the viewfinder window, and the cell is linked to a read-out on the top plate of the camera. SLR cameras usually employ cells positioned inside the camera body and only register light entering the lens. All exposure information is visible in the viewfinder, allowing the camera operator to concentrate on composition without looking away to check exposure. There are three main types of TTL metering systems: averaged metering, centre-weighted metering and spot metering.

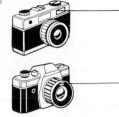

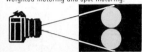

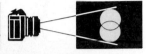

▲ **Averaged metering cameras** measure the light from both the top and bottom of the viewfinder frame. They work on the assumption that in most pictures there is an equal amount of foreground and sky and are therefore ideal for the landscape photographer. If used in the portrait (vertical) format they are not as accurate.

▲ **Centre-weighted metering cameras** have, like the averaged metering system, two areas of sensitivity, one at the top and another at the bottom. But in this system the two areas overlap at the centre of the viewfinder frame. The assumption with this system is that most people tend to position the object of most interest at the centre of the picture.

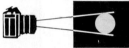

▲ **Spot metering cameras** are by far the most accurate of all the metering systems, and are to be found only on cameras manufactured in the past few years. They work on the same principle as hand-held spot meters, and measure light only from the very centre of the screen. If your subject is not at the centre, point the camera at your main subject, take a reading, set the exposure and then recompose your picture.

▼ **Taking a light reading in a backlit scene** can lead to exposure problems. The old rule about keeping the sun behind you when you compose a photograph does mostly work; but more interesting results can come from shooting into the sun. The problem in this type of situation is deciding what you are taking a picture of. In the shot below right, a light reading of the general scene led to a 2-stop underexposure of the principal subject. In the shot below left, the light reading was taken from the girl's skin. This resulted in a slightly over-exposed background but a correctly exposed main subject.

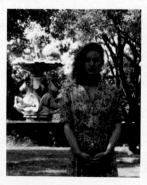

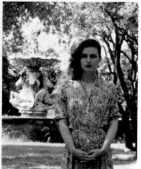

Lighting equipment

Indoor photography is most predictable when using tungsten lighting, as the effects of shadow and light, and their intensity, can be studied at leisure. When positioning lights use a dimmer switch to lower the light and heat output, prolonging lamp life and reducing discomfort.

1 Shallow-bowl reflector with cap
2 Flash umbrella
3 Standard reflector
4 Barn doors
5 Spotlight
6 Snoot
7 Studio flash

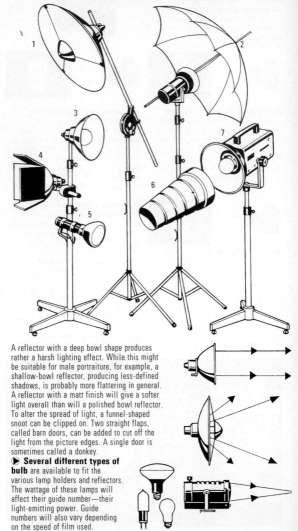

A reflector with a deep bowl shape produces rather a harsh lighting effect. While this might be suitable for male portraiture, for example, a shallow-bowl reflector, producing less-defined shadows, is probably more flattering in general. A reflector with a matt finish will give a softer light overall than will a polished bowl reflector. To alter the spread of light, a funnel-shaped snoot can be clipped on. Two straight flaps, called barn doors, can be added to cut off the light from the picture edges. A single door is sometimes called a donkey.

▶ **Several different types of bulb** are available to fit the various lamp holders and reflectors. The wattage of these lamps will affect their guide number—their light-emitting power. Guide numbers will also vary depending on the speed of film used.

▶ **Electronic flashgun units** are by far the cheapest and most portable type of artificial light source. A few non-electronic units are still available that take the old-style small clear or blue flash bulbs. The four-shot flash cubes are still used with many 126 and 110 format cameras.

Most electronic flashguns take from 4 to 20 seconds to recharge (or recycle) fully between pictures. Flash duration varies depending on type and may be as slow as 1/1000 or as fast as 1/50,000, so extremely fast action can be frozen irrespective of shutter speed. Many units are automatic and can be programmed just by dialling in your film speed and required aperture.

Some units also have a swivel foot so that you can bounce the light from the wall for a soft lighting effect. Others have tilting reflectors to bounce the light off the ceiling for the same soft effect. Yet other guns have a combination of swivel and tilt movements.

A few of the more complex amateur units even have accessories made for them as extras to vary the light quality. These may be coloured filters for special mood lighting effects, or wide-angle diffusers to spread the light so that it corresponds to the angle of coverage of a wide-angle lens. When buying a flash unit with a swivel head, make sure its automatic light sensor will keep pointing straight at the subject regardless of where the head is directed

1 Non-electronic flash
2 Flash cube
3 Front-swivelling flash
4 Tilting head flash
5 Clip-on reflector
6 Battery pack
7 Automatic flash with bounce head

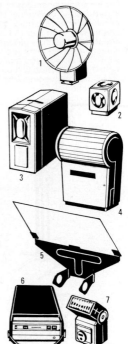

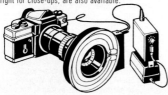

◀ **Holding the flash higher** and to one side gives better "modelling" (far left). Bouncing the light off a wall provides an even light (middle). Using the flash "on camera" 'left) gives a flat effect.

High-power electronic flash units are available to both the professional and keen amateur which run off mains electricity and recycle quickly. Output of these units is often variable. Ringflash units, which produce a shadowless, even, bright light for close-ups, are also available.

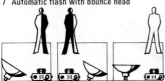

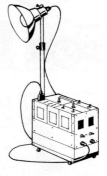

Accessories

For slow shutter speeds or time exposures the camera needs to be attached to some form of support, and tripods, with pan and tilt heads and legs braced to a geared central column, offer the firmest support. A monopod or table-top tripod used with a cable release will provide a less steady but more transportable combination.

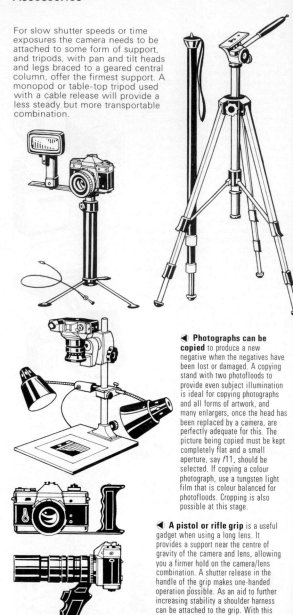

◀ **Photographs can be copied** to produce a new negative when the negatives have been lost or damaged. A copying stand with two photofloods to provide even subject illumination is ideal for copying photographs and all forms of artwork, and many enlargers, once the head has been replaced by a camera, are perfectly adequate for this. The picture being copied must be kept completely flat and a small aperture, say f11, should be selected. If copying a colour photograph, use a tungsten light film that is colour balanced for photofloods. Cropping is also possible at this stage.

◀ **A pistol or rifle grip** is a useful gadget when using a long lens. It provides a support near the centre of gravity of the camera and lens, allowing you a firmer hold on the camera/lens combination. A shutter release in the handle of the grip makes one-handed operation possible. As an aid to further increasing stability a shoulder harness can be attached to the grip. With this set-up shutter speeds as long as 1/4 should be possible.

The majority of picture-taking situations can be catered for with only a modest selection of prime lenses—a wide-angle lens, a standard lens and a not-too-powerful telephoto lens. However, the situation sometimes demands a more specialized lens. There are many on the market, but if you are not likely to make constant use of these lenses it is worth considering hiring as an alternative to buying.

1 A macro lens is designed to produce best results at extreme close range and can reproduce a subject up to life size. Macro lenses come in two basic focal lengths, 50 or 55 mm and 100 or 105 mm, and can be used for general photographic work.

2 A zoom lens has a variable focal length. This is achieved by constructing the internal elements so that some are movable and not fixed as in a normal lens.

3 A shift lens is a wide-angle lens designed for the 35 mm format. Part of the lens can be moved off its axis and therefore has the ability to correct the perspective distortion known as ''converging verticals'', common in architectural photography.

4 A bellows unit can be used with any lens to give a greatly magnified image, but a wide-angle lens is best because of its greater depth of field. This unit can provide greater-than-life-size magnification and infinitely variable magnification ratios.

5 A slide-copier is used in conjunction with a bellows unit to produce a duplicate slide or negative. A section of the original slide can be copied to fill the entire frame of the duplicate.

6 Extension tubes represent a cheaper alternative to the bellows. They provide a fixed distance separation between camera and lens for a fixed image magnification ratio. Extension tubes come in a set of three and can be used separately or in combination.

7 A lens hood fits over the front of a lens and prevents extraneous light from entering the lens and causing flare.

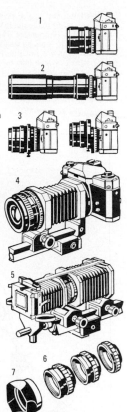

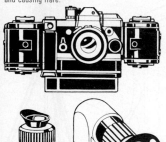

◀ **A motor drive unit** is an expensive item, but is used by most sports and press photographers to provide quick film advance between frames. Some units operate at five frames per second (fps), but most auto-winders operate at two fps.

◀ **A focusing magnifier,** which magnifies a small portion of the viewfinder's focusing screen, is very useful when accurate focusing is critical.

◀ **A right-angle finder** is used when the camera is in an awkward position, for example when the camera is on a copying stand or at ground level.

The studio/Design and equipment

For the keen still-life or portrait photographer, an area in the home set aside exclusively for equipment and models is desirable but probably impossible. But nearly any room, preferably with a north frontage, can be used as a pack-away studio. If permanent work surfaces are not practicable, then surfaces hinged to battens on the wall can be quite easily constructed. These can be fitted with collapsible or detachable legs, and when not in use the whole unit should sit neatly against the wall.

For most situations a selection of background papers, in a variety of lengths, widths and colours, is essential. These

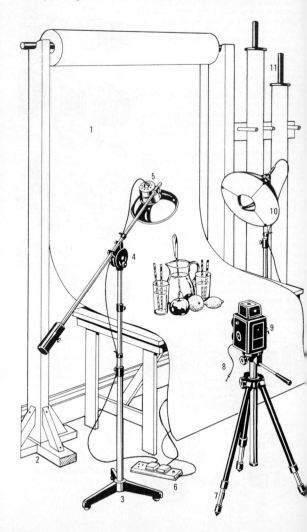

provide a plain, uncluttered backdrop against which to pose your subjects.

If you decide to go for small flash units instead of tungsten lights, try to avoid having extension leads trailing from unit to unit. If using daylight film, electronic flash can be supported by natural window light without presenting colour balance problems, and subsidiary flashguns mounted on slave units will do away with the need for connecting cables. All this equipment, as well as one or two tripods and a flash umbrella, should pack away into a convenient cardboard box.

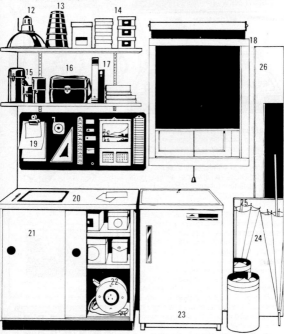

1	Background paper	15	Assorted lens cases
2	Support	16	Gadget bag
3	Adjustable stand	17	Files
4	Boom arm	18	Black-out blind
5	Shallow-bowl reflector	19	Notice board
6	Three-plug extension	20	Work surface
7	Tripod	21	Storage area
8	Cable release	22	Retractable extension lead
9	Twin-lens reflex camera	23	Refrigerator (for long-term
10	Shallow-bowl reflector with cap		storage of films and photographic
11	Spare rolls of background paper		paper)
12	Standard reflector	24	Reflecting flash umbrellas
13	Snoot	25	Mirror
14	Storage containers	26	Background flats

Storage and care

As equipment, negatives and slides start to accumulate, some form of storage and presentation system is vital. From the numerous types of cases, bags, files and magazines you are sure to find one that suits your needs perfectly. Even if your requirements are modest at the moment, the best system to invest in is one that can be added to over the years, so allowing you the possibility to expand.

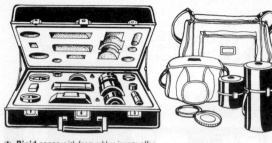

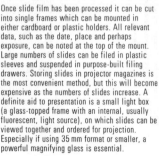

▲ **Rigid cases** with foam rubber inserts offer cameras and lenses the best protection. A lighter and cheaper alternative is the soft hold-all, but it is best to leave cameras, lenses and filters in their cases as an added protection against knocks. Always include as part of your kit a blower brush and lens cloth for on-the-spot cleaning of equipment.

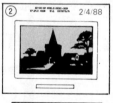

Once slide film has been processed it can be cut into single frames which can be mounted in either cardboard or plastic holders. All relevant data, such as the date, place and perhaps exposure, can be noted at the top of the mount. Large numbers of slides can be filed in plastic sleeves and suspended in purpose-built filing drawers. Storing slides in projector magazines is the most convenient method, but this will become expensive as the numbers of slides increase. A definite aid to presentation is a small light box (a glass-topped frame with an internal, usually fluorescent, light source), on which slides can be viewed together and ordered for projection. Especially if using 35 mm format or smaller, a powerful magnifying glass is essential.

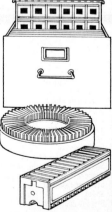

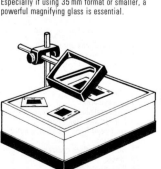

As a final check before loading slides into the projector a very convenient tool is the handviewer. These come in two basic types: viewers that need to be held up to the light to see the image and those with an internal light source (usually provided by two penlight batteries). For looking at a detail of a slide a small eyeglass is useful (these give approximately a x 8 magnification). Slide projector types are as varied as film formats. Most choice exists for those using 35 mm format film. If your budget is limited invest in a projector of modest specification only and use the money saved to buy the best possible lens. To project a large image in a limited space you will need a wide-angle lens, but if space is no problem a longer focal length lens can be used. The output of the projector lamp directly affects screen brightness, so ensure the lamp you buy is suitable for the viewing distance you will likely be using. As an additional extra some projectors can be fitted with a remote control device for automatic slide change and focusing. Any flat, white surface can be used to project pictures on to, but the most convenient surface is the fold-away projection screen. The screen is supported by a lightweight telescopic tripod and when collapsed the whole unit is very compact. The most reflective surface is the glass-beaded screen. This has minute glass beads incorporated on the surface, which reflect back nearly all the light falling on it. The problem with this type of screen is that the audience has to sit squarely in front of it. Strips of negatives need to be stored in a dry and cool environment or the emulsion will deteriorate. Special acid-free acetate sleeves are available to fit all film formats, which also ensure the successful long-term storage of negatives. Contact sheets and their corresponding negatives can be filed in ring-back folders. If storing slides in any form of box, try to include a packet of silica gel to absorb moisture.

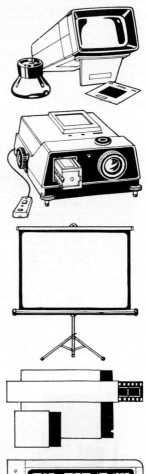

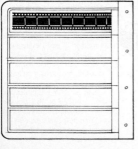

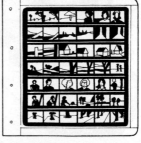

Film/Black and white film

Using the action of light to produce a permanent image was not possible until researchers in the latter half of the eighteenth century began to suspect that silver could be used for its image-forming properties.

Modern emulsions still use silver, or rather a compound of silver and a halogen (either iodine, bromine, chlorine or fluorine) which is later converted to metallic silver by the action of a developer. A thin layer of emulsion, containing the silver particles, is coated on to a plastic base. On the underside of the base is an anti-halation pigment, designed to stop light reflecting back from the near side of the film base.

The silver particles struck by the light entering the camera turn black when developed (representing highlight areas of the negative). Unaffected silver particles are removed during development, leaving the clear film base (representing shadow areas of the negative). At the printing stage, light from the enlarger shines through the clear sections of the negative and reacts with the silver compounds on the photographic paper; they turn black after development. But light cannot so easily pass through the developed silver of the negative, so leaving the photographic paper white. The grains (clumps of silver compound) of a negative are always the same size: the lighter or darker grey areas are simply a variation in the concentration of silver halides.

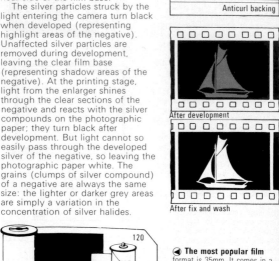

After development

After fix and wash

◀ **The most popular film** format is 35mm. It comes in a metal or plastic cassette in either 24 or 36 exposure lengths. Convenient and easy to load, disc and 110 films come in plastic cartridges, which are broken open to free the film for processing. All disc films have 15 exposures, but 110 (and 26) film has either 12 or 20 exposures. One of the most popular roll films is 120. 127 roll film is narrower, producing a picture format 42 × 42 mm. For the serious amateur and professional, 5 × 4 in (12.7 × 10.2 cm) sheet film is available. It needs to be exposed in a studio or view camera and comes in boxes of 10 or 25.

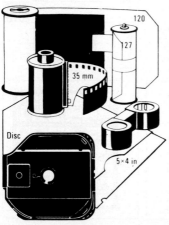

Four types of black and white film, each with a different ASA rating, were used to produce the accompanying photographs. All shots were taken with a Pentax and 135mm lens with the aperture set at f4. Shutter speeds were varied to compensate for the films' differing sensitivity to light. The first shot, taken with Pan F (50 ASA), shows the very fine grain response to be expected with this type of film. Skin tone is smooth and gradations of light and shade extensive.

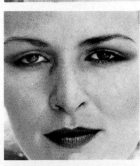

A medium-grained film, Plus-X (125 ASA), was used for this second shot. Skin tone appears coarser than before. Depending on size of enlargement and viewing distance of the final print, 125 ASA is probably the fastest film that should be used for head-and-shoulders portraiture.

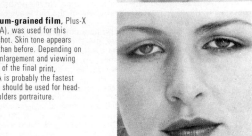

Tri-X (400 ASA) film was used to take the next picture. Apart from a further deterioration in skin tone the photograph lacks the sharpness and bite of the first two and many of the half-tones have disappeared.

I used Tri-X uprated to 1600 ASA for the final exposure. This represented a two-stop underexposure, which had to be compensated for in development. It is obvious that the grain response is now totally unsuitable for portraiture and the picture appears as if it has been printed with a texture screen over the enlarger lens. If used with discretion the type of effect caused by ''pushing'' film in this manner can create a very powerful, moody atmosphere.

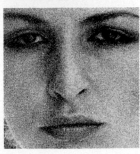

White light is the source of all colour, because it is a uniform mixture of all coloured light wavelengths. Each colour's light wavelength is measured in units called nanometers (one thousand millionth of a meter). The colours of the spectrum that are visible to the human eye range from deep purple (400 nanometers) to deep red (700 nanometers). Other light wavelengths such as infra-red and ultraviolet are actually outside the visible spectrum. Although the human eye cannot see ultraviolet light, films can "see" some light of this wavelength; this is why pictures taken in the shade or from a high altitude sometimes have a "cold" blue colour cast.

White light from the sun can be seen split into colours of the visible spectrum by allowing it to pass through a prism-shaped block of glass and on to white paper. With another prism, all the coloured light can be recombined into white light. We can see colours because objects reflect light of some wavelengths and absorb all others. A tomato reflects light of the red wavelength and absorbs other colours.

White light has three main or primary colours—blue, green and red. If you were to shine blue, green and red spotlights on to one surface, where all three overlap you will see white; where only two primary colours overlap, you will see a different colour, for example red plus green equals yellow.

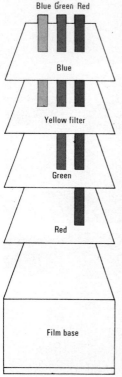

Blue Green Red

Blue

Yellow filter

Green

Red

Film base

Basically, a colour film is made of three layers of emulsion coated on a film base (see left). The top emulsion layer responds to and records blue, the middle layer records green, and the last layer records red. Originally a colour picture had to be made up from three different pictures—each made to record the red, green and yellow separately—which were combined for the total effect. With modern films this can be done with one exposure thanks to the carefully controlled multi-layer coating of film at the manufacturing stage. Colour films do not respond exactly like human eyes; a face appears to be virtually the same colour whether viewed in sunlight or indoors by room lighting. But not to a slide film. It is designed to respond to colours as seen by light of a certain colour temperature. Domestic tungsten lighting is more reddish than sunlight, which has a bluish quality. When using one type of film in the other light source, a colour-correcting filter must be used on the camera's lens.

Colour negative films, however, do not need this extra filtration, since any colour-cast can be corrected when the print is being made.

By placing a yellow filter immediately under the blue emulsion layer, blue, and especially ultraviolet, light is prevented from affecting the green and red emulsion layers. This yellow filter layer is destroyed later during the processing sequence.

Instant picture colour films are broadly similar, except that the dry-process films have layers of colour coupler and developer immediately below each colour emulsion layer. When the print is ejected from the camera, pairs of rollers squeeze the alkaline developing agent into the different emulsion layers. Meanwhile, an opaque top layer prevents daylight from reaching the (as yet) undeveloped images. This layer clears upon full development and the developing agent then forms a white layer behind the colour dye layers.

How colour film works

Two main types of colour film are available—one type provides a colour negative from which a colour print can later be made, and the other provides a direct colour positive image, or transparency, for viewing by transmitted light. Only recently have manufacturers made colour films (negative and transparency) with ASA ratings comparable with black and white emulsions.

Negative film

Colour negative film basically consists of three layers. As can be seen in the diagram, right, when light enters the lens and strikes the film, the blue component of light is stopped by the first blue-sensitive layer of the film. Green light is stopped by the second and red by the third. Yellow, for instance, being a mixture of green and red light, would be recorded by both the green and red layers but not by the blue. The action of light also forms a black silver image on development in all three layers. This is removed at the bleach and fix stage of processing, leaving the dyes incorporated in the layers unaffected. You have probably noticed that the colours of the negative are the complementaries of the colours in the original scene—blues appear yellow, greens appear magenta and reds appear cyan. This is because the blue-sensitive layer of the film carries yellow dye, the green-sensitive layer carries magenta dye and the red-sensitive layer carries cyan dye. The dye structure of the printing paper restores the colours of the original scene.

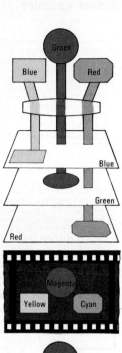

Transparency film

Transparency film must be exposed by a light source with a colour temperature for which it was designed—tungsten, photoflood or daylight. Once the film is developed colour faults cannot be rectified as they can with negative film. This is why exposure is of the greatest importance when shooting this type of film. Home-processing transparency film is now much simpler as new processing solutions only need to be kept at a little over room temperature. Transparency film is often called ''reversal'' because the image, once recorded (see right), must be reversed to restore the colours of the original scene. First the film is developed and then reversed (see below), followed by colour development and bleach and fix stages.

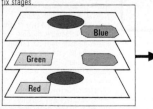

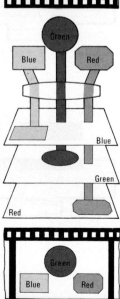

Reversing the image (above) can be achieved by re-exposing the film to light or by introducing a chemical agent in the colour developer.

Colour variables

There are many brands of colour film on the market, each with its own characteristics. Some will give you a result that is very close to the original; others may be very far from it. You can see from the eight examples on the right how colour can change depending on the film you use. The shots were all taken within a few minutes of each other under identical lighting conditions. Using a Pentax K2 set on automatic and a 50 mm lens. The difference is, however, only really apparent when you compare the results closely and for general use the results of most films are almost always acceptable. Remember, too, that processing can also make a huge difference to the result—if you had pieces of the same film developed in three different places you would end up with three distinctly different results. It is best to choose a film that suits your general requirements and to have it developed in the same place or process it yourself (see p.116). If home-processing, make sure you follow instructions to the letter, especially regarding time and temperature. It is interesting to note that different elements have come out better in different shots. The flesh tones are probably most successful in 1, the red in 6 and the blue of the flowers in 4. The best overall results have come from 1, 3, 6 and 7.

To get the best out of your colour film use it within the date stamped time limit and store it in a cool, dry place. For long-term storage of film many professionals keep it in a sealed container in the refrigerator.

When projecting slides, to get true colour make sure the projection lamp gives a clear white light and that the screen offers a clean white reflective surface.

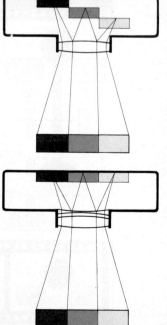

◀ **Chromatic aberration** is a lens's inability to bring all the coloured components of light into a single point of focus. White light, as we know from looking at the spectrum, can be split into seven main colour components. As each component enters the lens it is refracted, or bent, to a different degree—much as a stick entering a pool from various angles seems to be bent to different degrees. The top diagram, left, shows light entering a simple camera lens. The red constituent of light comes to a point of focus at the rear film plane, while the blue component is focused closest to the lens, with green falling between them. In a photograph, this type of lens would produce colour fringes, especially noticeable around highlights. By using a type of lens called an achromatic doublet (lower diagram, left) the colours can all be brought into focus at the film plane. The achromatic doublet is constructed using two types of glass, each with a different refractive index (or ability to bend light). Strictly speaking, an achromatic doublet will only bring two colours to the same point of focus—usually blue and green. The third colour, red, is already correctly focused.

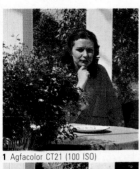

1 Agfacolor CT21 (100 ISO)

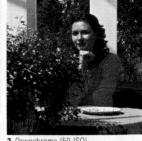

2 Orwochrome (50 ISO)

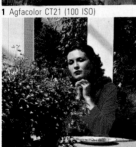

3 Sakuracolor (100 ISO)

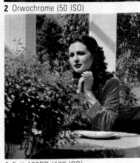

4 Fuji 100RD (100 ISO)

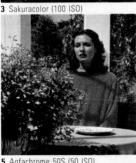

5 Agfachrome 50S (50 ISO)

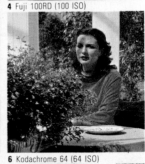

6 Kodachrome 64 (64 ISO)

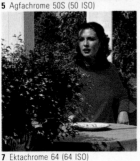

7 Ektachrome 64 (64 ISO)

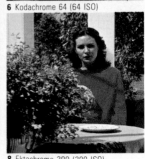

8 Ektachrome 200 (200 ISO)

Using the camera

Whenever possible it is best to load the camera indoors, where there is less possibility of grit or grime entering the delicate mechanisms exposed when the camera back is open or of stray light fogging the film. If the camera must be loaded outdoors, stand with your back to the wind to create a pocket of relatively still air. To safeguard against scratched negatives, do not remove the film from its sealed container until just before loading; dust can easily become lodged in the light-tight velvet trap of the cassette and thus cause long scratches or tracks when the film is advanced or wound back.

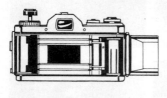

◀ **Open the camera back** and, before loading the film, inspect all the exposed surfaces for dust. Ensure the film guide rails and the film pressure plate (found on the back of the camera) are free from grit. Dust can be removed using a blower brush (preferably with the bristles removed) or with the ragged end of a torn lens tissue.

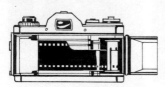

◀ **Remove the cassette** from its sealed container and slot it into the camera compartment. Pull the tapered film-leader out and insert it into the take-up spool, making sure it is firmly attached. If the leader becomes free the film will not advance, and film will be wasted.

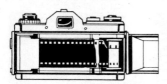

◀ **Once the film is firmly secured** on the take-up spool, advance the film, either manually or by moving the film-advance lever, until the leader disappears and the sprocket holes (both top and bottom) engage with the geared spool. Check to see the film is running square on the guide rails, close the back and advance the film twice.

To make the most of every picture-taking opportunity requires a degree of routine. A wrongly set film speed, a badly focused image or inadequate depth of field are a few of the factors resulting in disappointing photographs.

Ensure the film is winding on properly—the rewind handle should spin as you advance the film.

Set the ISO number on the camera's film speed dial or separate hand-held meter (see p.18).

Check there is enough power in your camera or light meter batteries.

Familiarize yourself with the type of metering system used in your camera or meter (see p.19).

Check highlight and shadow areas of the scene you want to photograph to ensure contrast range is not too much for the film to handle (see p.38).

Select shutter speed—ensure it is fast enough for hand-holding or use a camera support (see p.22).

Select aperture—if your camera has a stop-down button check to see if depth of field is adequate (see p.36).

Focus the image and shoot—bracketing exposures for important photographs.

Incorrect focusing and incorrect holding of the camera can result in very similar problems—indistinct and fuzzy images. Manufacturers of 35 mm system cameras produce a variety of different focusing screens to suit most tastes and circumstances, including microprism, split-image and ruled-grid screens, especially useful for ensuring verticals and horizontals are true in architectural photography. People with poor eyesight can fit correction lenses to the viewing window of the camera. Rangefinder cameras usually give you a secondary ghost image, which aligns with the main image to indicate the point of focus.

▶ **Camera design** usually dictates the most convenient way of holding and focusing the camera. Grip the camera securely, but not too tightly, with your right hand, leaving your index finger free to trigger the shutter release. Your left hand is now free to adjust not only the focus ring but also the aperture ring and shutter-speed ring or dial. Extra stability can be given to the camera if you press it lightly against your face. Once you have finished adjusting the camera's exposure and focusing, place your left hand, especially if using a long lens, under the lens to cradle some of the weight. At all times try to adopt a relaxed position.

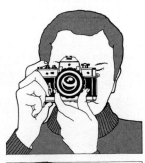

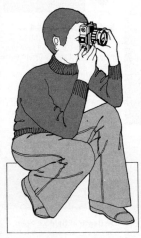

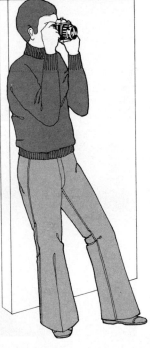

▲ ▶ **Different positions** demand different techniques. Crouching to take a picture does not differ markedly from the technique described above, but if you are using the camera in the vertical format, rest your right elbow on your knee for additional support, as shown above. Quite slow shutter speeds can be used if you can find a convenient wall or other support to lean against to stop your body swaying (see right).

Focusing and aperture

Out-of-focus pictures often result not from setting the focus ring at the incorrect mark but from camera shake. Lightweight 110 and 126 format cameras need careful handling as the slightest movement caused by depressing the shutter release results in blurred pictures.

There are occasions when critically sharp images are not desirable. Soft-focus lenses or lens attachments are available to intentionally diffuse an image, creating a more flattering photograph.

Both pictures below were taken at f1.2. For the first shot I focused on the eyes, and depth of field is so shallow the girl's hair is just out of focus. The second shot is deliberately out of focus to show how light and shade have merged.

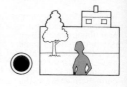

For any lens there is only one point of true focus. Around this point is an area—known as the depth of field—where the image, although not in true focus, is acceptably sharp. Depth of field is variable and changes depending on the aperture and focal length. For the shot on the right I used an aperture of f2 on my 50 mm lens. Depth of field at this aperture only covers the girl.

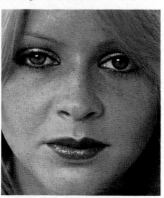

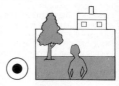

▶ **An aperture of f5.6** was used for the next shot, still using the same lens. It can be seen that at this smaller aperture more of the frame is acceptably sharp, with depth of field extending into the middle distance. This photograph and accompanying diagram illustrate the point that the smaller the aperture the greater the depth of field.

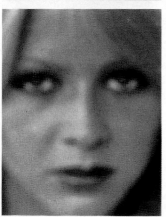

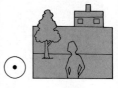

▶ **Depth of field** has been even further extended in this final photograph. Taken with the diaphragm closed down another two stops to f16, the picture shows that at this aperture depth of field ranges from only a few feet in front of the camera to infinity (see also diagram). It is possible with very wide-angle lenses not to bother with focusing at all, as the depth of field at every aperture is so extensive.

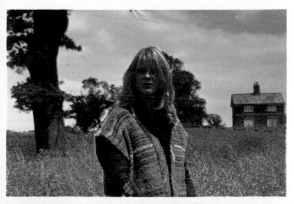

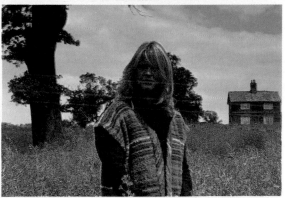

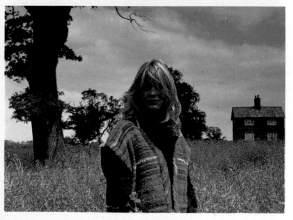

Exposing/Black and white

Gauging exposure is the most difficult task confronting the camera user not working with a fully automatic camera. Every photograph is a mixture of light and dark—highlight and shadow—and a light reading taken from one area alone can lead to serious exposure problems for the other.

Modern exposure meters (see p.18)—either selenium cell or CdS—can be relied upon to give accurate readings in most situations. They are at their best in flat, even lighting where there is minimal variation in tone or contrast. Problems arise, however, when a light reading taken from a highlight indicates more than a two-stop difference compared to a reading taken from a shadow area in the same scene. This type of situation is not all that uncommon and although the eye can easily cope with the contrast levels, it needs careful observation for you to be able to recognize scenes with contrast levels that might prove troublesome for the film you are using, and to compensate for them. Beach scenes in bright sunlight, indoor shots with strong sunlight filtering down through high windows, ground-level scenes overhung by leafy trees creating areas of intense shadow and bright highlight all represent potential problems.

All film has some degree of contrast latitude—black and white negative film having the greatest range, followed by colour negative film, with colour reversal film needing the most accurate exposure—but once this two-stop difference between highlight and shadow is exceeded a decision usually has to be made either to expose for the shadows and allow the highlights to burn out, or to expose for the highlights and let the shadows become solid. (For tips on selective printing of enlargements see p.115.) A less contrasty scene will probably benefit from an averaged reading of highlight and shadow.

The two pictures opposite are good examples of high-contrast scenes where contrast itself has been used to create evocative images. I took the picture of the girl in a nightclub using available light only—a table-lamp. The contrast was already interesting so I exposed for the highlight in order to dramatize the face looming out of the darkness. Crisp winter-morning light and a dark-clad figure presented a dilemma in the picture below. Finally I decided to expose for the highlight and made a note to increase development by 50 per cent to extend contrast.

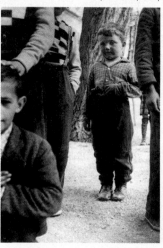

A situation may dictate your exposure. Not wanting to disturb the mood of the group, left, I could not ask the boy I wanted to photograph to change his position to make the lighting effect more favourable. In this type of situation you can use an average reading to give some detail in both shadow and highlight areas, expose for the highlights and let the shadows go dark or expose for the shadows and burn out the highlights. I chose the last option and exposed for the shadows—this gave detail in the clothes but meant that the face and the foreground burned out a little.

◀ *Rolleiflex, 80 mm, HP5, 1/125, f8.*
▼ *Minolta, 135 mm, Tri-X, 1/30, f4.*
▶ *Nikon, 50 mm, Tri-X, 1/125, f8.*

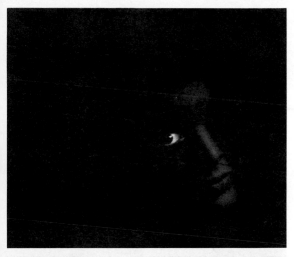

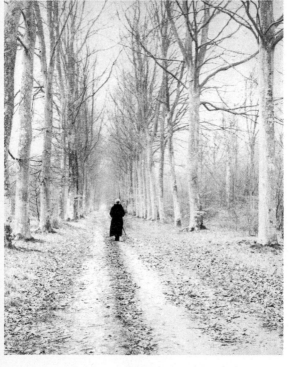

Exposing/Colour

Exposing colour film involves as much care as does exposing black and white film. Even professionals will admit to disasters in this area, and the problem is compounded by the fact that there is no *correct* exposure. Depending on whether you want a high-key or low-key picture, exposure, for the same subject, can vary by up to four or five stops between the brightest highlight and the deepest shadow. For a uniformly exposed picture, flat, even lighting is best as the one- or two-stop difference is well within the contrast range of negative film and just within the capabilities of slide film.

The seven exposures presented here show that varying the exposure affects not only definition and mood but also colour. Three of the shots are acceptable, but the middle one is probably best, showing good detail in highlight and shadow. *Pentax, 55 mm, Ektachrome 64, f1.2-f16.*

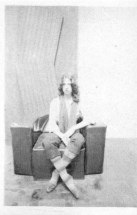

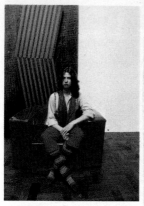
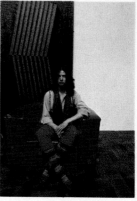

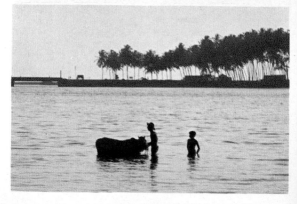

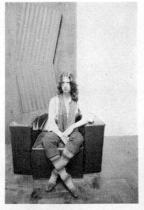
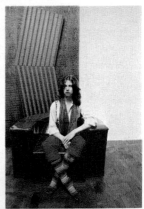
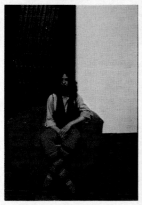
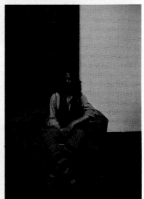

▶ **Deliberate underexposure** can be used for special effects. In the moonlit picture of a girl posing on a chair, right, underexposed two stops, so the delicate highlight reflected from her white lace dress seemed to glow in the darkened surroundings. *Hasselblad, 80 mm, Ektachrome 64, 1/250, f16.*

◀ **Deliberate overexposure** can also be used to make a more personal statement about your surroundings. When I came across the pair, left, watering and bathing their cow I was struck by the simplicity of the composition formed by their presence and the line of trees and buildings on the far shore. To avoid cluttering the picture with unnecessary detail I overexposed by three stops. *Rolleiflex, 80 mm, Ektachrome 64, 1/250, f8.*

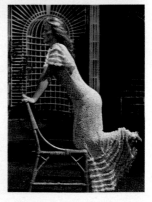

Principles of selection

When selecting subject matter for a photograph make sure you capture your point of interest in the simplest way and present it in such a way that it conveys the effect or emotion you are looking for. By your chosen angle of view, careful juxtaposition of images and attention to lighting you can create pictures to heighten the viewer's perception. Removing extraneous detail often gives greater impact to the subject. In many cases a detail speaks with greater intensity than a photograph of the whole subject: the wrestler, below, is a case in point. Here the tension of the struggle is conveyed by the selection of a detail expressive of the whole scene; we do not need to see the whole figures in the ring to be able to imagine them.

▼ **By coming up close** to the horse, below, instead of taking a standard middle-distance shot, I have given it stunning visual impact. Had I taken the shot from a greater distance the horse would have looked much less impressive and the eye would have been distracted by the landscape. I positioned the shot so the shape of the skyline echoes the back of the horse.
Hasselblad, 60 mm, Tri-X, 1/125, f16.

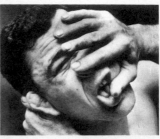

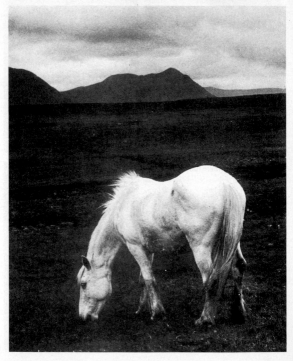

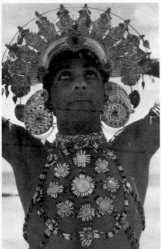

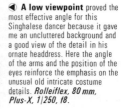
◀ **A low viewpoint** proved the most effective angle for this Singhalese dancer because it gave me an uncluttered background and a good view of the detail in his ornate headdress. Here the angle of the arms and the position of the eyes reinforce the emphasis on the unusual old intricate costume details. *Rolleiflex, 80 mm, Plus-X, 1/250, f8.*

▶ **Physical distance** serves to draw attention to distance in years in the portrait of father and son, below left. I emphasized physical differences by keeping the boy in the foreground in soft focus, which shows off the smoothness of his young skin in contrast with the weatherbeaten, experienced face of the older man. Notice how the lines of the stone in the background echo the lines on his face. *Hasselblad, 150 mm, Plus-X, 1/250, f5.6.*

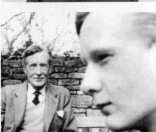

▼ **Spontaneous actions** can sometimes confound your careful selection of images, offering you something even more effective; you need to stay alert to all the possibilities. I was originally concentrating on the shadow cast by Henry Moore's sculpture, ''King and Queen'', below, when the sculptor himself walked by. His presence unified the group and added a new dimension to my first composition. *Rolleiflex, 80 mm, Tri-X, 1/250, f16.*

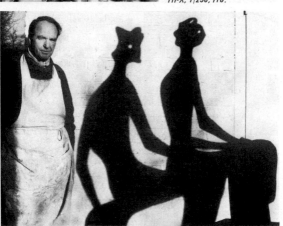

Composing

By arranging the elements of
your picture you manipulate
subject matter to express a
particular point of view. Vertical
lines take the eye into a picture;
horizontals across it. By making
full use of perspective you can
get a three-dimensional feeling.
Composition will vary depending
on whether you are using black
and white film stock or working
in colour.

▶ **Time of day** can influence
composition; in the evening light, right,
the long shadow emphasizes the figures
and defines the area in which they are
standing. The bright colour against the
sombre background ensures that the
isolated figures stand out. *Pentax,
100 mm, Agfachrome 50S, 1/250, f8.*

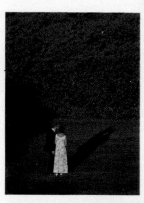

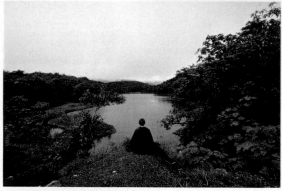

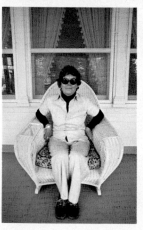

▲ **The landscape** dictated the
positioning of the figure, above. The
strong triangular silhouette in the
foreground leads the eye forward into the
heart of the landscape and the circular
shape of the water takes the eye round the
detail at the edges of the composition.
Both shapes are strong visual elements in
any composition; judicious use of such
shapes can make your pictures much more
interesting. Because the picture was taken
in the rain there is poor saturation in the
colours. *Pentax, 28 mm, Agfachrome
50S, 1/60, f11.*
◀ **Objects** can impose a certain
composition. The wicker chair on the
balcony, left, was under the window when
the woman came and sat herself in it in a
pose which at once echoed the symmetry
of the composition but, in its rigidity,
provided a contrast to the overall leisurely
atmosphere. *Leicaflex, 35 mm,
Ektachrome 64, 1/60, f8.*

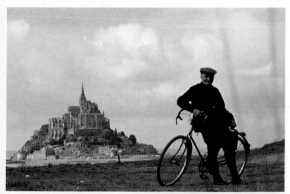

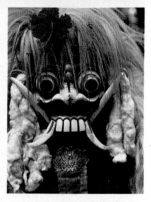

▲ **Harmony of shape** unites the cyclist and the outline of Mont St Michel, above; this is further emphasized by the inverted pyramid of space between them. *Contax, 35 mm, Ektachrome 64, 1/250, f11.*

▶ **Close-ups** need composing no less carefully than other shots. Your cropping decision depends on the mood you want to create, but by coming in close you need to generate some excitement or impact. In the picture of the mask, right, the shape of the face and the tusks has dictated the framing. *Pentax, 100 mm, Ektachrome 64, 1/125, f11.*

▼ **To position a silhouette** of the funeral procession, below, on the skyline, I lay in the grass because standing with the camera at eye level I lost the mourners behind the trees. *Hasselblad, 80 mm, Ektachrome 64, 1/250, f8.*

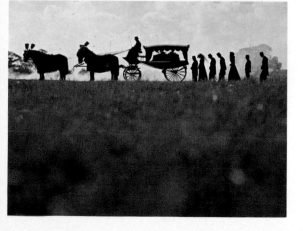

Background, middle distance and foreground

One of the best ways to produce a three-dimensional effect is to make calculated use of background, middle distance and foreground. If you can make a link between these areas of your photograph an illusion of depth will immediately be created. When composing try to organize the images so that the main subject is stressed and the others are played down.

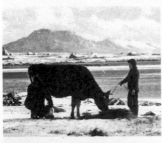

◀ **The foreground** can be used to dominate the picture, as in the photograph of the Hebridean scene, left. The strongest image in the picture is in the group with the cow, which firmly registers the importance of the foreground; middle distance and background fade away, bringing out the bleakness and isolation of the area. *Vivitar 35EF, 28 mm, Plus-X, 1/250, f11.*

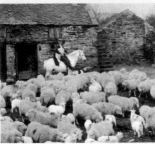

◀ **A continuous link** from foreground (sheep), through middle distance subject (shepherd) to background (stone walls) can be made by subject matter, texture and form. *Pentax, 28 mm, Plus-X, 1/125, f8.*

▼ **Background** is of primary importance here, although the chorister in the foreground provides a subject link with the chapel. Diminishing size creates a sense of distance and gives scale to the building. *Hasselblad, 80 mm, Plus-X, 1/60, f11.*

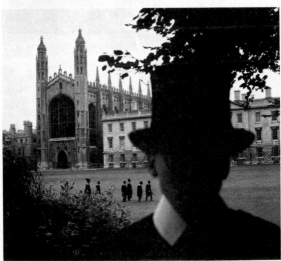

▶ **A simple device** for linking foreground and distant subject matter is to shoot through a window, long grass, trees or a gate, as in the picture of Bombay, right. This gives a sense of perspective to the picture and can give a feeling of voyeurism to the viewer. It is very often used to good effect by professional photographers. *Pentax, 50 mm, Plus-X, 1/250, f16.*

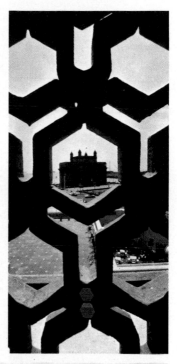

▼ **All the elements** in the photograph of Singapore Harbour, below, are of equal importance. Linking the old boats in the foreground to the skyscrapers behind is the river, which gives linear perspective to the picture, taking the eye right to the heart of it. This composition makes an interesting social comment on the contrast between the bustling, traditional life seen on the boats and the monied modern conditions reflected by the buildings behind. It is the selection and juxtaposition of such images that distinguishes the caring photographer, who will produce the really competent, aware photograph, from the casual snapshot merchant. *Pentax, 28 mm, Plus-X, 1/125, f11.*

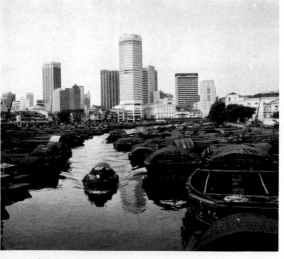

Shape, pattern, texture and form

You can find these elements in most photographs, whether they are highly subjective or simply serve as a record. To improve your understanding and appreciation of composition it helps to try to isolate and exaggerate these elements and to take some photographs that emphasize their individual qualities. Concentrate on one element at a time.

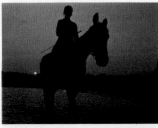

◀ **Shape** has probably the strongest visual impact of all. Although there is no detail in this picture we have no difficulty in recognizing horse, rider or trees. The evening sun sets the mood and introduces enough colour to evoke an emotional response. Outline and silhouette provide enough additional information. *Leicaflex, 135 mm, Ektachrome 64, 1/125, f16.*

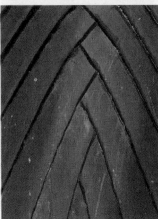

◀ **Pattern** has a flattening effect on pictures, although there is some form in this palm leaf. Highlight and shadow have given surface interest to the leaf, but the predominant effect is one of a flat area of pattern. *Pentax, 100 mm macro, Ektachrome 64, 1/125, f11.*

▼ **Repetition** is not necessarily an ingredient of pattern; the effect can be kaleidoscopic as in the range of fabrics, below. Although there is texture in the picture it is dominated by large areas of colour which produce the overall effect of a flat image. *Pentax, 100 mm, Ektachrome 64, 1/60, f11.*

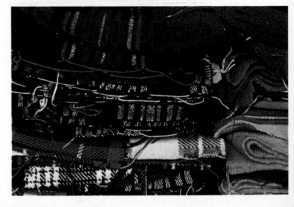

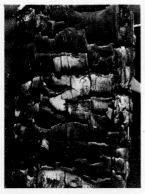

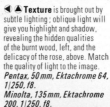

◀ ▲ **Texture** is brought out by subtle lighting; oblique light will give you highlight and shadow, revealing the hidden qualities of the burnt wood, left, and the delicacy of the rose, above. Match the quality of light to the image.
Pentax, 50 mm, Ektachrome 64, 1/250, f8.
Minolta, 135 mm, Ektachrome 200, 1/250, f8.

▶ **All photographers** strive to capture form, to give an impression not just of surface but of substance. Light the image to emphasize the direction of the form; diffused directional light is the most effective. Make sure the shadows are underneath or you will produce an effect that does not look real.
Contax, 135 mm, Ektachrome 160, 1/60, f8.

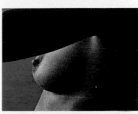

▶ **Subtle form** calls for subtle lighting. Contrast gives the illusion of depth; juxtapose hard and soft surfaces, plain and patterned, light and dark, bright and sombre. The lighting of this textured binding emphasizes the quality of the form rather than the surface.
Pentax, 100 mm, Ektachrome 64, 1/125, f8.

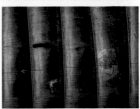

▶ **All the elements are balanced** in this harmonious composition of a traditional pottery. All the shapes are easy to read and, although individual elements could have been photographed very differently, collectively they all show up well. Many people have an intuitive understanding of these basic elements, but it is often necessary to isolate them in order to respond to them individually. If you examine the photograph you can see how different areas could have been treated. Here there is nothing to distract the eye from the simple, continuous tonal range of colour.
Pentax, 28 mm, Ektachrome 200, 1/250, f16.

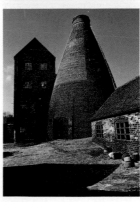

Step-by-step photography

If you have to dismantle complicated machinery, need to keep a record of intricate processes or have to give precise, step-by-step explanations, the camera is invaluable. The aim is to impart information and your technique should be correspondingly straightforward and consistent. Try to use uniform lighting, similar camera angles and the same film stock. Use a tripod and mark its position if you are photographing over a period of time. If you are taking slides for projection keep the image size constant as far as possible.

(All pictures) Pentax, 35 mm and 50 mm lenses. Ektachrome 64, around 1/125, f11.

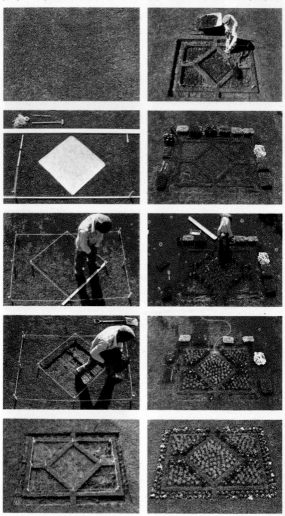

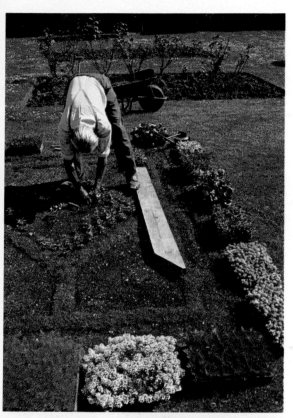

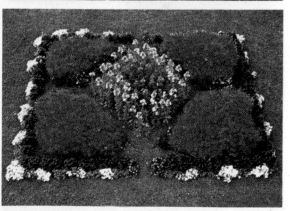

Time of day

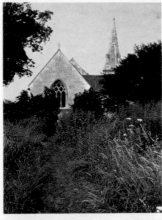

Light changes colour and intensity throughout the day and during the course of the seasons; it can alter the appearance of a building, picking out intricate details at one moment, obscuring prominent features the next. I photographed this isolated church on a summer's day to demonstrate the great variety in mood and composition that one location can offer.

◄ **7.00 am.** Sunlight begins to filter through, giving weak directional light and slight modelling. *(All pictures Pentax, Ektachrome 64); (left) 35 mm, 1/125, f8.*

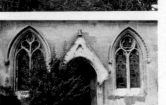

◄ **8.30 am.** The sun is a little stronger now even though there is still some cloud; it is giving greater modelling to the architecture and providing a strong contrast between the texture of the church wall and the foliage. I chose to come closer to the building than for the earlier picture, as the diffused sunlight was ideal, giving form and modelling to the facade. *50 mm, 1/125, f16.*

◄ **10.30 am.** The sun has now moved round to the south picking out the main porch. The intricate detail in the stonework is clearly defined and the rich colour of the tiled roof shows up well. *100 mm, 1/250, f11.*

▼ **12.30 p.m.** In the midday light the main entrance can be seen to its best advantage. *35 mm, 1/250, f16.*

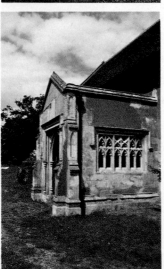

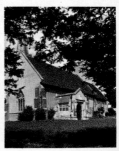

▶ **2.30 pm.** The sun moving towards the west throws light over the length of the building and the grassy graveyard, relating setting to church. Include some figures in shots of architecture as they lend a sense of scale. *28 mm, 1/250, f16.*

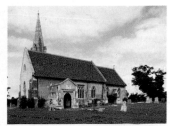

▼ **3.30 pm.** The afternoon sun on the tower made this the best time to capture its architectural detail. *28 mm, 1/250, f8.*

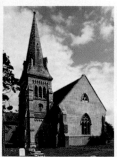

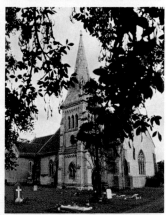

▶ **5.00 pm.** As the light had started to fade by now I introduced some foliage into the composition to give some tonal contrast with the building. *28 mm, 1/250, f16.*

▼ **7.00 pm.** Rich evening light made this the best time to take the church from a distance to give an impression of its fertile agricultural environment. *35 mm, 1/125, f11.*

▶ **9.00 pm.** The intense colour of the setting sun contrasts with the silhouette of the church, and all detail is lost. *400 mm, 1/500, f5.6.*

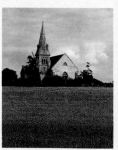

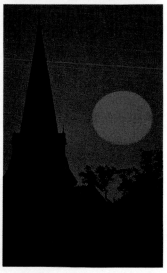

Weather

So many people take photographs in high summer in harsh midday sunlight. These conditions are bad for most things: early morning, late evening, cloud, and even rain and mist offer excellent possibilities. Use existing light to capture the prevailing atmosphere, as in the summer storm, right. Under these conditions, keep your camera ready for the fleeting rainbow. In fog or mist, familiar objects, like the boat, below, take on a new identity, with subdued; colours and softened shapes; colour film today can reproduce infinite subtleties.

▶ *Pentax, 135 mm, Ektachrome 64, 1/250, f 5.6.*
▼ *Leicaflex, 400 mm, Ektachrome 200, 1/250, f 8.*

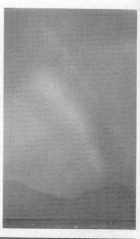

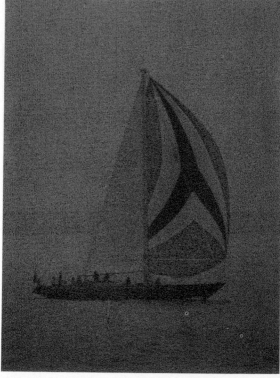

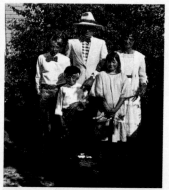

◀ **Harsh sunlight** is not very flattering as this joke picture of a family group shows. It is particularly difficult to photograph people under these conditions. All the eyes are squinting, the faces are almost obliterated, the shadows are hard and unkind and there is a general lack of detail. However, the picture is effective in its own way because it is aiming to record the overall atmosphere of a hot summer day rather than to portray a group of individuals. *Minolta, 55 mm, Ektachrome 64, 1/500, f 11.*

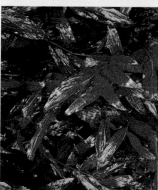

◀ **Make the most of rain** because it brings life and brightness to dull surfaces like roads and roofs; the leaves, left, have become shiny and reflective. Shelter under an umbrella and don't worry if your camera gets a little wet—but dry it as soon as possible. *Pentax, 100 mm, Ektachrome 64, 1/60, f 4.*

▼ **When photographing in snow,** take a light reading off your hand or grey card, as you may be misled by light bouncing off the snow. Use a UV filter to cut haze and produce crisp outlines. Choose viewpoints that offer a contrast; here you have hard rocks and soft clouds. *Minolta, 135 mm, Ektachrome 64, 1/500, f 16.*

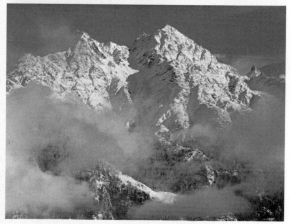

Strong natural light

While it is very sound general advice to keep the sun to one side behind your shoulder, shooting into the sun or back-lighting can give you an exciting explosion of light. However, if you include the point source of light it burns out and desaturates all colours; if you expose for this rest of the picture will be in darkness; the trick is to make sure the sun is judiciously positioned behind an appropriate object. Take light readings at right angles to the light source to get comparative densities.

▶ **Sunset or sunrise** is the best time to use the sun as back-lighting, when it is low enough to be partly obscured by the people or objects in your photograph. To take the girl, right, I exposed to give good detail in the shadow area, allowing the light to burn out her head. *Minolta, 55 mm, Ektachrome 64, 1/125, f 5.6.*

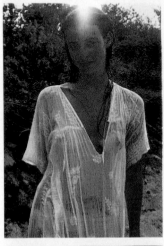

▼ **The point source** of light has been lost in the glowing portrait of a teaching monk, below, but light from the setting sun has flooded into the room and reflected back on the people in it. To capture the detail indoors I took a light reading from the middle boy's shirt. When you are shooting in reflected light, the colours come closer together. *Rolleiflex, 55 mm, Ektachrome 200, 1/60, f2.8.*

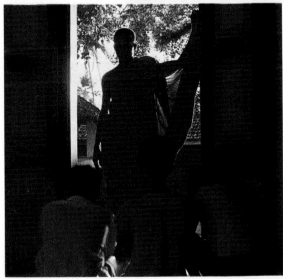

▶ **The way light falls** on an object can completely change its colour and appearance. These two pictures of balloons were taken within minutes of each other but in opposite directions. Above, the light falling on the balloon makes everything in the picture, including the basket, very sharp and brings out the strong colours and the contrast with the bright blue sky. Below, the colour is much weaker, the detail is lost and the emphasis is on the silhouette. The colour is particularly subdued here because the light is going through two thicknesses of material. *Pentax, 100 mm, Ektachrome 64, (above) 1/250, f11, (below) 1/500, f16.*

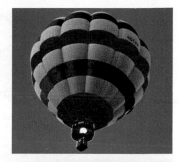

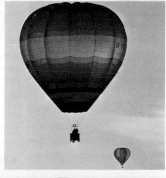

▼ **Brilliant sun** will flare into the camera lens and give ghost images of the iris diaphragm on the film if you shoot towards it. You can see this in the camera and shoot accordingly (it will reduce image quality). Remember that it is very dangerous for your eyes to point your camera at the sun. *Rolleiflex, 55 mm, Ektachrome 64, 1/250, f8.*

Colour filters

A few of the many colour filters available can be seen grouped on the right. Used alone or in combination they can remove reflections, penetrate haze, give colour spot or graduated effects, or balance film stock to light source. For details of colour and special-effects filters see pages 132-3.

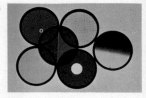

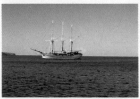

◀ **Taken without a filter** this straight-forward picture of a yacht at anchor, left, is a good example of the type of picture that can benefit from filters designed to alter both colour and atmosphere. All pictures were taken within a few minutes using a Pentax, 55 mm, Ektachrome 64, 1/250, f8. For each exposure only one filter was used, but to multiply the effects more than one filter can be used.

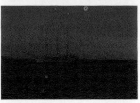

◀ **The green and yellow dual-coloured filter** used for the picture on the left makes no concession to reality, and its very strong, unnatural coloration tends to swamp the subject. I positioned the filter so that most of the yacht appeared against the yellow and not the stronger green. Also, the yellow produced a better horizon effect than did the green.

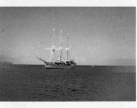

◀ **The graduated filter** used left is dark brown at the top, becoming lighter towards the centre of the frame. The other half of the filter is clear glass. I used this filter to try and add a little atmosphere to a rather featureless expanse of blue sky, making it appear much more ominous and threatening than it did in the first picture. I could have rotated the filter to reverse the colour effect.

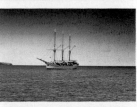

◀ **A diffusion (or soft-focus) filter** has subtly helped to change the atmosphere of this version of the photograph, without adding any exaggerated colour effects. This filter has a clear central area, so anything positioned at the middle of the frame is not affected. The wider the aperture the greater the effect. You can get the same effect by smearing grease or petroleum jelly on a plain glass filter.

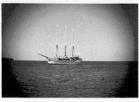

◀ **A coloured filter** with a clear central spot leaves the middle of the frame as it would appear naturally, but produces a coloured vignette at the edges. Apart from funnelling attention to the centre of the picture, it also implies that the yacht is being observed from the circular port hole of another vessel. As with the dual-colour filter used above, the effect of the colour-spot filter is limited.

▶ **A "colorburst" diffraction** filter was used (right) to change this straight-forward street scene into a multitude of dazzling lights. This filter does not need any exposure adjustment as it does not exclude any light. Its kaleidoscopic effect comes from its ability to split light into its separate colours. *Nikkormat, 50 mm, Ektachrome 200, 1/60, f5.6, "colorburst" filter.*

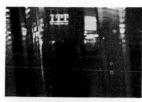

▶ **Without the addition of a "vario-starburst" filter**, the shot of a darkened headland (right) would have appeared flat and uninteresting. Instead, this filter has picked out the brightest point sources of light and spread their rays into brilliant star patterns, giving a point of interest to the composition and balancing an otherwise featureless frame. *Pentax, 55 mm, Ektachrome 200, 1/30, f4.*

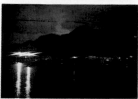

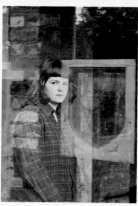

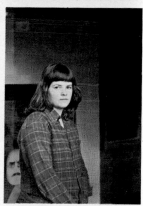

▲ **The two photographs above** show the effect of a polarizing filter. In the first shot a confusion of main image partially obscured by prominent reflections can be seen. For the second shot I attached a polarizing filter and rotated it until most of the reflections had been eliminated. Because this filter does remove some light, a two-stop exposure adjustment was necessary to avoid underexposure.

▶ **Infra-red light** (right) produces bizarre colour distortions in familiar objects. An infra-red transmitting filter can be used to block the longer wavelengths of light, and because the effects of this type of film are unpredictable, a strong yellow filter should be used to generally warm up the colours. Vegetation tends to reproduce as magenta, reds go yellow, skin tones go greenish and blacks go maroon.

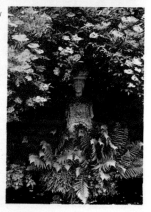

Mixing light

You can greatly extend the range of creative opportunities with colour photography if you experiment with different types of film in different types of lighting. Daylight film is matched to daylight at noon and has a blue quality; used in artificial light it increases the orange and gives a warm effect. Tungsten film is matched to artificial light and becomes bluish in daylight. The normal procedure is to select your film according to which kind of light predominates. In a daylit room, for instance, a small area under a table-lamp can become a beautiful orange highlight if shot with daylight-balanced film.

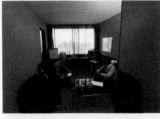

◄ **Daylight film** has given a warm glow to the interior, left, because it was lit by artificial light. You can, however, see the daylight, which is bluer, through the window. This shot and the two below show how you can vary the appearance of the same scene by using different film in different conditions. *(All pictures) Pentax, 21 mm, (left) Ektachrome 200, 1/15, f16.*

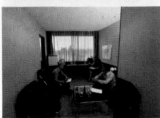

◄ **Tungsten film** has rendered the same interior much greener. It was taken in the same lighting conditions. The light is now much nearer the true colour but there is a predominant cast, which gives a rather chilly atmosphere. *Ektachrome 160, 1/15, f11.*

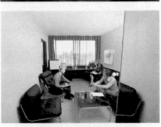

◄ **Electronic flash** matched to daylight film has given the truest result in available light. However, each of the three pictures on its own would probably be considered acceptable. *Ektachrome 200, f16.*

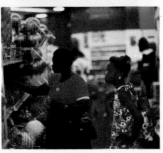

◄ **Fluorescent lighting** does not really present problems even though it restricts the colour range. There are filters available to correct the colour balance but I consider the difference so slight it is hardly worth using them. Remember to use daylight film if in white (natural) light, artificial light film if in yellow or pinkish (artificial) light. This will give you an acceptable colour rendering of most subjects you will encounter. *Pentax, 55 mm, Ektachrome 64, 1/30, f4.*

▶ **Dramatic effects** can be achieved with fireworks or other moving lights if you hold the shutter open for a while. Here I captured the effect of several rockets at once by exposing for 18 seconds, during which time they were set off continuously. I covered the lens between rockets to avoid the intrusion of local light. *Pentax, 35 mm, Ektachrome 64, 18 sec, f16.*

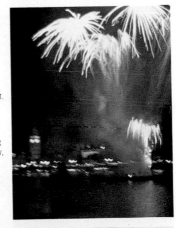

▼ **To capture the movement of the car lights** at dusk, below, I put the camera on a tripod and waited for the car to move off. I calculated that it would take 30 seconds for the car to pass me and adjusted the aperture accordingly. *Rolleiflex, 80 mm, Ektachrome 64, 30 sec, f16.*

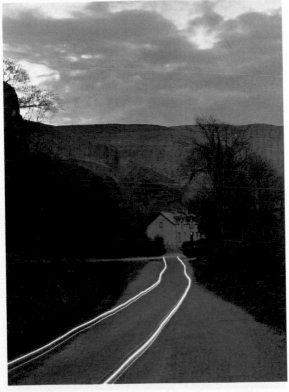

Available light

While it is true to say that any photograph taken without supplementary lighting is taken in available light, we usually mean by this term pictures taken in poor light and without flash. The advantages are that you capture more of the atmosphere and get a more subtle light: flash tends to give a harsh light in the immediate area, throwing the rest of the picture into darkness.

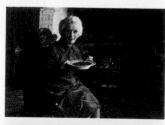

◀ **Firelight** can be soft and flattering as it is in the portrait, left, where it is combined with side-lighting to bring out the detail. By exposing for the shadows I have made the room look much lighter than it was. People look and feel relaxed in available light and are not disturbed by the unnatural brightness of flash.
Pentax, 50 mm, Agfachrome 50S, 1/30, f8.

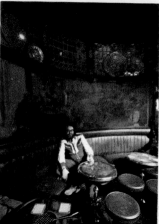

◀ **A shaft of light** can be used to pick out the subject. The poet Adrian Henry, left, stands out of dark surroundings, where the colours offer no reflected light. Take advantage of available light in all public interiors, particularly where people are performing or speaking, so you do not distract or disturb anyone. *Pentax, 28 mm, Ektachrome 200, 1/15, f4.*

▼ **Gloomy light** often produces pictures rich in fully saturated colours. Notice how this girl's eyes and teeth gleam and how the lack of light has contributed to her lack of self-consciousness. I positioned her head in a gap in the busy background and exposed for the highlights.
Pentax, 55 mm, Ektachrome 200, 1/30, f4.

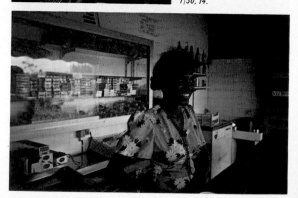

▶ **Candlelight** is quite harsh, but the movement of the flames gives a softened effect. You can also get interesting pictures that are a faithful record of what the eye sees by using the light of a match or torch. *Vivitar, 50 mm, Ektachrome 160, 1/15, f2.8.*

▼ **Modern film** can capture subtle detail in a poorly lit subject; notice the quality of this boy's skin and trousers, textures barely visible with the eye. Fast film and fast lenses are often a great asset; don't make the mistake of not taking them because you are going to a hot climate. *Pentax, 28 mm, Ektachrome 200, 1/30, f4.*

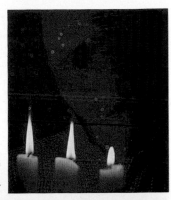

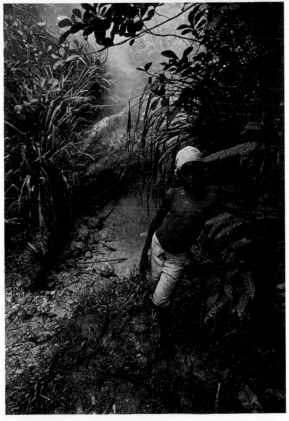

Photographing the subject

Each photograph you take should have an individual point of view; this does not mean that you will want to look for a contrived effect but simply that you should examine all the possibilities of the subject and come up with the most appropriate interpretation. Spend as much time as you can before you shoot, looking hard and exploring alternative viewpoints; consider different lighting arrangements and details of composition. Very often quite commonplace objects or events can be given a new significance by the angle of view that you choose, the juxtaposition of unexpected images or a revealing emphasis of detail. Consider also time of day and the effects of light and shade as a creative device.

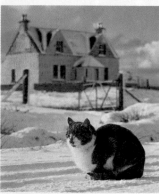

◀ **Always be on the look-out** for the unexpected. The photograph, left, has a bizarre quality due to the cat's apparent relaxation in the snow. The camera angle for the cat and its home was achieved by my lying flat on the ground in the snow. *Pentax, 55 mm, Ektachrome 200, 1/250, f8.*

▼ **The appropriateness of the image** below made me take this photograph of a wine-growing estate reflected in a glass of the wine produced there. By inverting the order in which one would expect to see the images, I stressed the importance of the produce. *Mamiya, 180 mm, Ektachrome 64, 1/250, f8.*

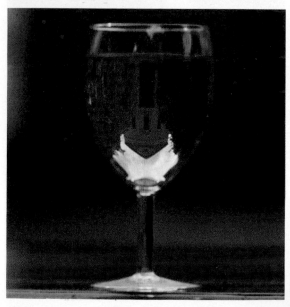

▶ **Time of day** can sometimes be used to introduce an unexpected element. To photograph this rugged castle in its romantic setting I got up at dawn to capture the early morning mist and deserted landscape and get a romantic effect. In places frequented by tourists it is always a good idea to have an early start before people and cars arrive. *Contax, 135 mm, Tri-X, 1/250, f8.*

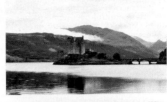

▶ **By obscuring the face** you depersonalize the human form. By placing the girl, right, behind the lampshade, I have made her body simply one of several intriguing elements in this composition. *Pentax, 35 mm, Plus-X, 1/15, f8.*

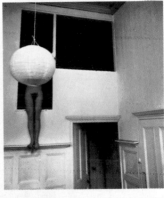

▼ **By drawing attention to significant features** you can highlight important aspects of a person's life and work. Barbara Hepworth, below, was sitting under a roof light with her hands highlighted when I came to photograph her. I emphasized them further by using a wide-angle lens. *Hasselblad, 50 mm, Tri-X, 1/30, f8.*

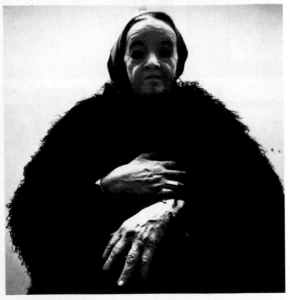

Still life

You can learn a lot from still-life photography; working with inanimate objects gives you complete control over composition and lighting. Plan your shot, then collect more objects than you aim to use; build around the largest or most interesting. Always check the effect through the camera. Plain or textured backgrounds are best. Use simple lighting for a three-dimensional aspect with shadows going in one direction: diffused daylight with a white card reflector, or one light, possibly with a bounced fill-in light to soften shadows and give detail. Use a tripod and slower fine-grain film. Shutter speed is not critical so try to get everything sharp by using a small aperture.

▼ **Glass** is fascinating to photograph as it is so responsive to lighting conditions. Here are two straightforward ways to treat it. The bottles and glass below have been back-lit by light bounced off the wall behind to give a silhouette, with a side-light and reflector to add detail. In the composition, bottom, I used a side-light with a curved reflector on the opposite side to give delicate high-key reflections. Sometimes simply using available light from a window gives the most satisfying and subtle effects. Remember that glass demands a very accurate exposure. *Linhof, 100 mm, Tri-X, (below) 1 sec., f22, (bottom) 4 sec., f16.*

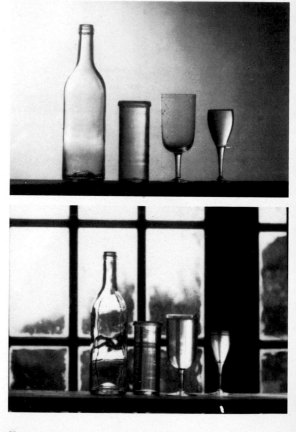

▶ **Simple shapes** such as the basket, right, show how a tonal range can give the illusion of form. Here a soft directional light with a reflector has provided the necessary modelling. By aiming for a negative of medium contrast you will get a wide range of control when printing. *Linhof, 100 mm, Plus-X, 1 sec., f32.*

▼ **In composite still-life** pictures the objects should relate to each other; they may be of similar shape or colour, belong to the same period, or, as with the bookbinding equipment, below, to the same trade. I used daylight and a reflector here, but a photoflood behind a white sheet would have done. *Linhof, 65 mm, Plus-X, ½ sec., f 16.*

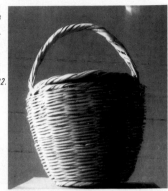

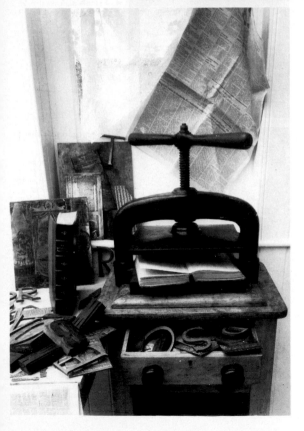

Food

For photography food should be in peak condition. Fruit and vegetables should be hand-picked; if you want to cut them in half do it just at the last moment. Remember that lights and sunlight dry food out, so turn on lights at the last minute or, if possible, use electronic flash. Cook food for about two-thirds of the usual cooking time so that shapes are retained and then photograph immediately. For a shiny appetizing surface brush with oil or glycerine, where appropriate. If a dish might spoil, use a substitute while you finalize details of composition and lighting; when you are taking the real thing you must work quickly.

For complicated shots work out your composition first. You can use a background for a special effect in a way that complements the food and extends the possibilities of still-life photography (see below, right). However, it is usually best to use a plain background that does not compete with the food. Select props that harmonize in colour and shape If your photograph cuts into objects in the foreground you will give a feeling of immediacy.
▶ *Linhof, 65 mm, Ektachrome 64, f16, Balcar electronic flash.*
▶ *MPP, 80 mm, Ektachrome 64, 3 sec., f16.*

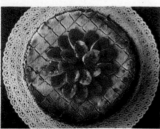

◀ **A single dish** can show all the subtleties of good cooking. Be careful not to get shadows of yourself or your camera in the way. For close-ups I underexpose $\frac{1}{2}$ stop on transparency film for greater colour saturation. *Pentax, 100 mm, Agfachrome 50S, 1/30, f5.6.*

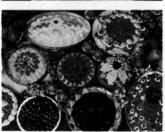

◀ **Food prepared for special occasions** deserves to be recorded. The time you spend on lighting and composing the shot should reflect the time and effort that has gone into the cooking and preparation. Diffused daylight is good for dishes that are subsequently to be eaten. The best flat surface is the floor; get up above your composition on a stepladder. *Pentax, 35 mm, Agfachrome 50S, 1/30, f5.6.*

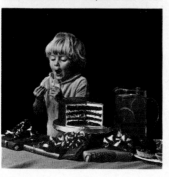

◀ **Food makes a good prop** for pictures of children. The boy, left, photographed at his birthday party, was quite unselfconscious as he played with the candles on his cake. For this type of shot it is useful to use flash to arrest movement; here I managed to get the effect of diffused daylight by using a flash reflected off a white sheet with another white sheet used to give fill-in light. If possible, always position the flash near a source of natural light to avoid cross-shadows.
Rolleiflex, 55 mm, Ektachrome 64, 1/60, f8.

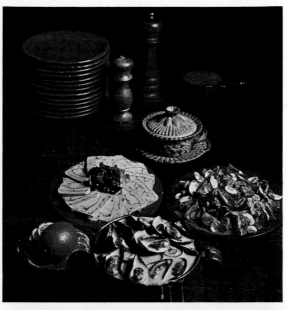

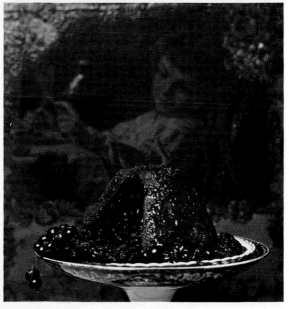

Portraits

The first consideration of portrait photography is to bring out character. Lighting, though all-important, is secondary. Where appropriate use soft directional light for a flattering effect. North light is ideal. Talk to your sitter to establish a relationship; if possible, let people continue their work as you photograph them.

Sometimes unconventional lighting, as in the portrait of Henry Moore, right, can be effective. I wanted to capture his mood of concentration and let the back-lighting emphasize the strength and sensitivity of his hands. *Hasselblad, 150 mm, Tri-X, 1/125, f5.6.*

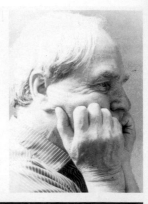

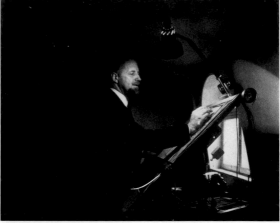

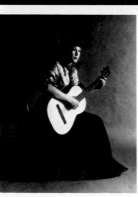

▲ **Light from a single point source** can be overwhelmingly harsh. To photograph Basil Spence, above, at his drawing board, in the light of an Anglepoise lamp, I turned the light to the wall to put him in reflected light and to reduce contrast. *Pentax, 55 mm, Tri-X, 1/30, f2.*

◄ **Both girl and guitar** are important in the portrait, left. Here dramatic lighting suggests a stage performance: I lit a grey paper background from the side with a diffused 1000-watt spotlight; white studio walls provided fill-in light, giving detail in shadow areas and lessening contrast. It was worth taking some time to arrange this shot so that the girl was comfortable and could sing in a relaxed way. *Hasselblad, 80 mm, Tri-X, 1/25, f8.*

▶ **Faces can be used** for emphasis, as in the magazine photograph, right, where the eyes, looking down, draw the viewer's attention away from the face and towards the brooch. The strong frontal lighting minimizes the features so that the symmetry of the composition is immediately noticeable. Beauty photographs are very often lit in this way as frontal lighting eliminates skin flaws. I used a black velvet background and put the girl in a black velvet cape to absorb all light. When you need to double expose, black velvet absorbs the most light. *Hasselblad, 150 mm, Tri-X, f16, Balcar electronic flash with a white umbrella next to the camera.*

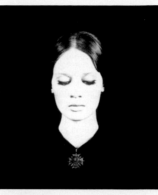

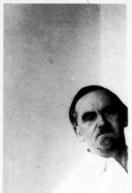

▲ **In the studio** of William Scott the painter, above, I noticed that the light on the various white surfaces gave different shades of grey, an effect characteristic of his work at the time. To give the impression he was superimposed on one of his canvases, I photographed him behind a door. *Bronica, 80 mm, Tri-X, 1/60, f8.*
▶ **I posed** the two close friends, right, in front of a window and stood in front of them, careful not to block the light. For lively and spontaneous pictures, put the camera on a tripod so you don't have to talk to people from behind the camera. *Bronica, 80 mm, Tri-X, 1/60, f8.*

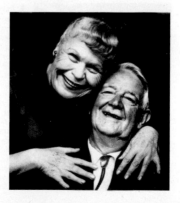

Portraits out of doors

When photographing people out of doors, it is necessary to give greater emphasis to the person than to the environment. Then, if you have selected an appropriate angle, or by using selective focusing, you can combine both elements successfully. The characteristic portrait of Graham Sutherland, right, was taken while he was studying the light on a thornbush. The tangled undergrowth and the dappled light contribute to an atmosphere of quiet contemplation but do not compete with the artist. More uniform lighting would have highlighted unwanted detail.

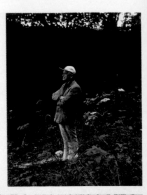

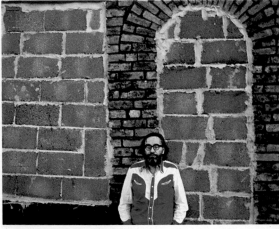

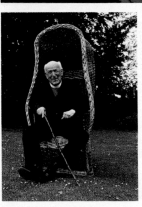

▲ **Relationships in shape and colour** can form interesting links between subject and background. I photographed the poet Adrian Henry outside the house where he was born, above, in evening light. This produced a blue cast in shadow areas and emphasized the blues behind and in his clothes. By sheer coincidence there are also strong similarities between the shapes on the building and on his clothes. *Pentax, 100 mm, Ektachrome 64, 1/30, f8.*

◄ **Props can be used to tell a story.** I photographed the former Archbishop of Canterbury, Dr Fisher, after he retired; the wicker chair seemed to express his increased leisure time, while its style lent dignity. *Rolleiflex, 50 mm, Ektachrome 64, 1/125, f8.*

▶ **A formal pose** can be made more interesting by the angle from which you shoot and the introduction of other elements to contribute to the story. I shot from a diving board to get a clear background for the contest winner, right. *Minolta, 35 mm, Agfachrome 50S, 1/250, f5.6.*

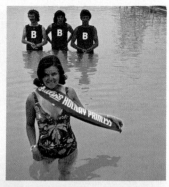

▼ **Looking straight into the camera** draws the viewer's attention as in the compelling portrait of two Malayan dancers, below. Tropical vegetation provided a suitable background against which to contrast the subtle skin tone. *Pentax, 100 mm, Ektachrome 64, 1/125, f8.*

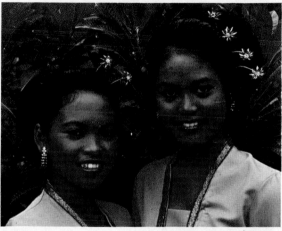

▶ **Natural poses** are a help to the photographer. The gardener, right, adopted this stance as we chatted and as it expressed his personality and aspects of his work I asked him to hold it. I exposed for shadow detail, which enabled me to capture his rugged complexion. Shooting slightly against the light can give interesting modelling in portrait photography, although, of course, if you shoot directly against the light you may get little more than a silhouette. This effect is helped here by the pyramid composition, in which the man's face forms the centre of interest. *Rolleiflex, 50 mm, Ektachrome 64, 1/60, f8.*

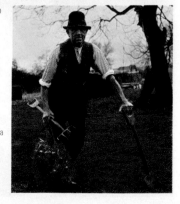

Portrait variations

Seeing how many different character pictures you can get of the same person is a good exercise in portrait photography. Actors and actresses make good subjects as they are unselfconscious in front of the camera. You can easily get hold of props such as wigs, false beards, moustaches and glasses at theatrical costumiers. Try them in different permutations and let the sitter assume an appropriate pose for each. Use soft, directional light and a plain background for additional flexibility.
(All pictures) Hasselblad, 150 mm, HP5, f16, electronic flash.

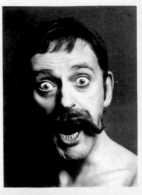

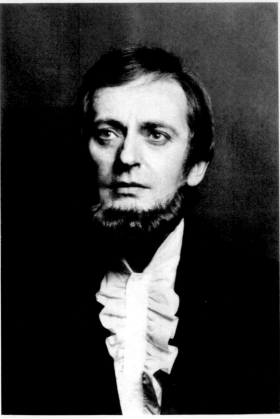

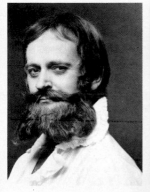

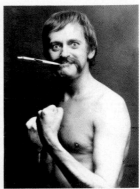

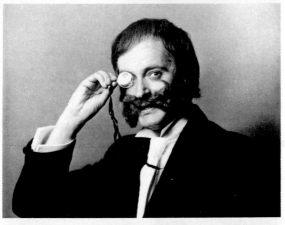

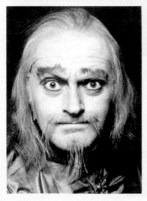

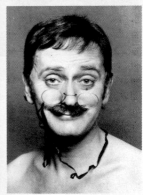

Character portraits

If you possess a camera with fast lenses, i.e. f1.2-f2.8, and use fast film, you will be able to do portraits indoors in existing light. This is very useful as you may find that there is nowhere else available but in any case your subject will always feel more relaxed at home or in a familiar situation. This applies particularly to elderly people and young children. Often a tripod is desirable for shots of 1/15-1 sec. or more—this will enable you to get photographs with relatively little light. If you haven't got one to hand you can wedge your camera against a wall or rest it on a suitable surface. Practise at home, with your own family.

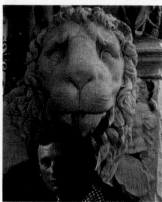

◀ **An intriguing effect** has been achieved in the portrait of Patrick Proctor, left, by combining the subject, lit from the left by an Anglepoise lamp, with a poster of the Arsenale in Venice, which was taken with lighting from the right. The relative size of the images adds to the interest of the composition. Their juxtaposition is particularly appropriate as Venice inspires much of the artist's work. Had I been unable to find an appropriate poster of Venice I could have achieved a similar effect with front projection (see p.98). *Vivitar 35EF, automatic, Ektachrome 64.*

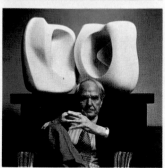

◀ **Hand-holding the camera** was possible, in the portrait of Henry Moore, left, as his studio was a very light working space. I photographed him as he was relaxing after finishing some drawings. The different colours you can see in the background add interest to the composition; the walls were painted different colours for the sculptor to view his work in various situations. *Rolleiflex, 80 mm, Ektachrome 64, 1/125, f8.*

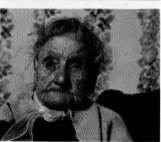

◀ **To photograph old people** (Mrs Aida Rowe, left, was 113) you should leave them in their own surroundings: don't disturb them with a lot of equipment and bright lights. The old lady's room was small and dark, so I used a tripod and a time exposure. This gave very faithful colour. *Rolleiflex, 80 mm, Ektachrome 64, 2 sec., f4.*

▶ **Colour casts**, such as the yellow glow, right, can create an atmosphere; here the excitement of a party in a marquee. If I had tried to filter it out I would have got artificial colour and lost the real record of the event. As it is, the warm glow over the whole picture reinforces the boy's party mood and cheerful expression. *Pentax, 55 mm, Ektachrome 64, 1/30, f2.*

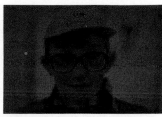

▶ **Light rooms** with white walls give a perfectly even, balanced light suitable for flattering portraits. There is plenty of modelling but little shadow in the gentle portrait of the girl, right. Beauty shots are often taken in similar situations. *Hasselblad, 150 mm, Ektachrome 64, 1/250, f8.*

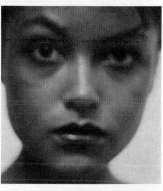

▼ **Harsh midday sunlight** is usually bad for portraits. However, it gave appropriate modelling to the Zulu woman, below, and brought out the rich colours in her costume. *Rolleiflex, 80 mm, Ektachrome 64, 1/250, f16.*

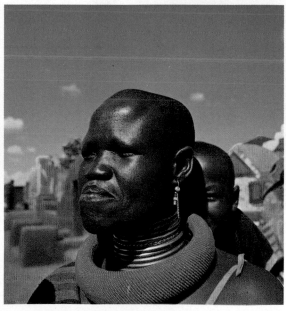

Nudes

Photographing the nude gives you the opportunity to show form in many different ways, from the abstract to the sensuous. Lighting is the key to the mood you create.

For inexperienced models use natural light as I have in the gentle portrait of a pregnant woman, right.

Details of the human body can form dramatic and unusual compositions. The hand, below, emerging from and returning to darkness gives a surreal effect. Normally light should follow the shape of the body, but breaking the flow of the form by shadow can produce interesting results.

▶ *Linhof, 80 mm, Tri-X, 1/30, f5.6.*
▼ *Hasselblad, 150 mm, Royal-X, 1/30, f5.6, illumination from a 100-watt electric light bulb.*

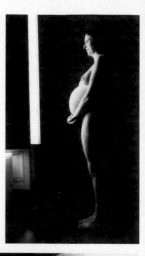

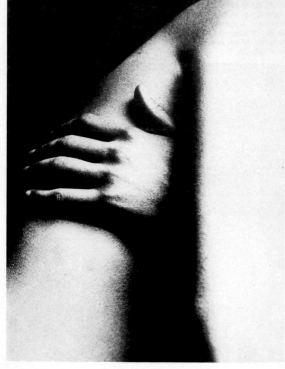

▶ **To bring an element of chance** into nude photography it is worth experimenting with electronic flash as I did here, or using a slow shutter exposure to capture some movement. You can also get interesting results from out-of-focus images, where the image moves across the picture or towards the camera, or by using reflections. Settings for nudes can range from the highly ornate and evocative to the plainest possible background with no props at all, right. Whether the result is romantic or purely abstract is very much up to the photographer, who, in this kind of photography, has enormous scope for bringing in his own ideas. For a spontaneous effect like this you must use models who are quite unselfconscious without clothes and who move well. *Hasselblad, 80 mm, Tri-X, f11, Balcar electronic flash.*

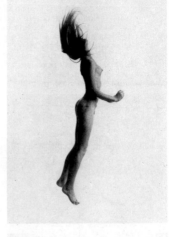

▶ **Controlled lighting** has separated the planes, right, and subtle variation in lighting between figure and background has brought out the form. I used two diffused floodlights next to the camera and two more on the background behind the figure. *Hasselblad, 150 mm, Tri-X, 1/60, f5.6.*

▼ **The provocative study,** below, was taken in early morning light, which has given tremendous clarity to the corn and wild flowers as well as sharp form to the body. To create a romantic atmosphere I could have used soft-focus filters or petroleum jelly. *MPP, 180 mm, Tri-X, 1/250, f11.*

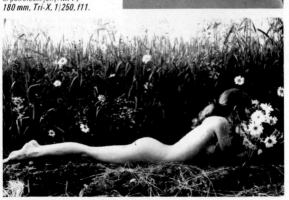

Children

Children are among the most difficult but most rewarding of subjects for photography. The main problem is persuading them to keep still, so rule out elaborate lighting systems and pre-focusing. To give them the freedom to move around use overall lighting such as photofloods reflected off a white ceiling or sheet. Flash can be useful but don't fire it into a child's face as it can be both frightening and distracting. Remember that children get bored easily and may not want to participate for more than a few minutes at a time, so keep your camera handy and loaded with fast film for non-flash pictures.

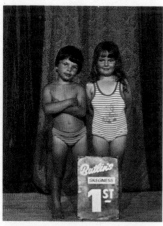

◀ **Special events** in children's lives should always be recorded. To get the best results at prize-givings and other ceremonies you will have to behave like a press photographer—proud parents are unlikely to be refused permission. Try to include some of the background or general setting to bring out the atmosphere and to help you remember the event in later years. The card in front of the beauty contest winners, left, tells the story of the event. Because the children were posed I could use a relatively slow exposure in the existing light, which was a mixture of fluorescent light and spotlights that reproduced the atmosphere of the event much better than flash would have done. *Vivitar 35EF, automatic, Ektachrome 64.*

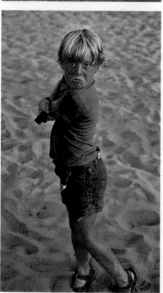

◀ **Fleeting expressions** have to be captured quickly and it is sometimes impossible to focus accurately or to work out the exposure in time. It is better to get the picture even if it is slightly out of focus than to lose the moment altogether. In my haste to catch the boy's grimace, left, I cut off part of his feet. Remember that keeping a real record of your children involves all the temper and tears as well as the smiles and happy moments. *Pentax, 50 mm, Ektachrome 64, 1/250, f4.*

▶ **Set everything up in advance** for studio shots so you don't keep children waiting and try to keep them amused. Even so you may find a young model walks out on you as mine did here, providing me with an interesting character shot. However, after behaving badly for some time, he suddenly decided, as often happens, to be thoroughly co-operative. *Mamiya, 135 mm, Agfachrome 50L, f16, electronic flash.*

▶ **Babies** are happiest when they are nude and free to kick and wriggle, so this is a good time to take pictures of them. Apart from close-ups of faces, which all parents want, it is interesting to record stages of development and involvement with surrounding objects. Keep backgrounds clear and don't include anything not relevant to the picture; in the light nursery, right, all I needed to do was take a picture off the wall to create an ideal setting for this relaxed picture. *Vivitar 35EF, automatic, Ektachrome 64.*

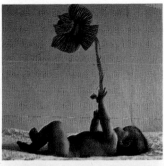

▶ **By kneeling down** you can take children at their own level and often get a clearer background as well. The boys, right, were quite happy to pose because they had a new toy. By using a wide-angle lens I made the boy in the foreground, who was taking the lead in the game, look more dominant than the boy behind. The striped sweater emphasized this effect. Shooting in diffused evening sunlight against a shadow area has provided good contrast. *Rollei, 55 mm, Ektachrome 64, 1/250, f2.8.*

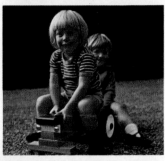

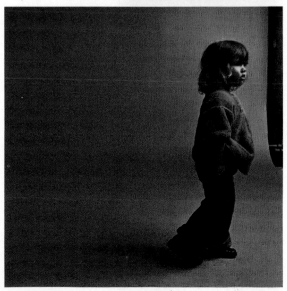

Groups and events

Social and sporting events account for so many photographs that it is always worth doing some homework first. Go to the location, look at the space available, colour and lighting conditions, and appropriate backgrounds; make sure you have permission to photograph if necessary. Use fast film and lenses of appropriate focal length and position yourself so you do not distract the people you are photographing.

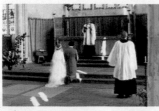

Wedding photographs cannot be repeated! Plan in advance to avoid mistakes. On this occasion I went to the church first to check the lighting, get permission and establish that I could hide behind a column in order not to disturb the service—had this been a problem I would have tried to shoot from the balcony using a tripod.

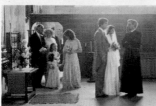

▼ **Special moments** such as the blessing (top) can only be captured if nobody is disturbed. I positioned myself out of sight and used a wide-angle lens.

◀ **Informal moments,** such as preparing to leave the church (above left), are often the best. When people are concentrating on their role in the event they are unlikely to feel self-conscious.

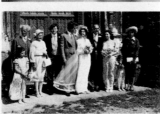

◀ **Group shots** are a must— but they need not be rigid and lifeless. I find the moments just before and just after the "official" pose give the best results—leave two or three exposures to use when the group thinks you have finished. *Pentax, 28 mm, Ektachrome 200, (first 2) 1/30, f3.5, (third) 1/500, f11.*

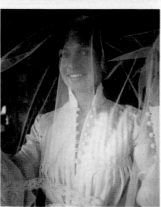

◀ **Close-ups** are an important part of the record of any event. I photographed the bride, left, while she was arranging her veil in a mirror. As she was concentrating on what she was doing she did not feel—and consequently did not look—self-conscious. My 135 mm lens enabled me to take the picture without getting in her way. Use a long lens for this purpose or to isolate detail in a crowd from a distance. *Pentax, 135 mm, Ektachrome 200, 1/125, f2.5.*

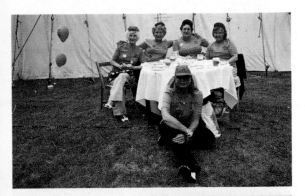

▲ **Let people pose
themselves** and you will get an
informal picture. Although the
composition is formal the mood
of the participants is relaxed.
*Vivitar 35EF, automatic,
Ektachrome 64.*

Sporting events offer dramatic
subjects who are not inhibited by
the camera. To isolate the skater,
right, I chose a slow shutter speed
and panned; that gave the feeling
of movement and obliterated an
irrelevant background. To capture
the atmosphere of the hunting
scene, below, I compressed the
group by using a longer lens.
▶ *Pentax, 100 mm, Ektachrome
200, 1/30, panned, f16.*
▼ *Pentax, 135 mm, Ektachrome
200, 1/250, f11.*

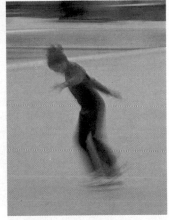

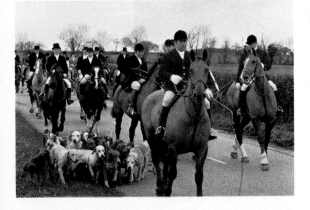

Travel

You will be more comfortable if you travel light, but try to be prepared for most eventualities. Use a strong camera bag and take 3 lenses, if you have them, lens cleansing material, lots of film, a spare battery for your meter and a supply of plastic bags. Make notes on all the shots you take—including general historical or geographical information as well as all the relevant technical details. When you return don't have all your film processed at once—send some out for testing first to make sure there is nothing wrong that could be corrected in the processing.

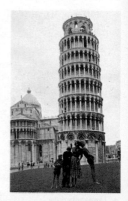

▶ **Even traditional tourist spots** taken with family groups can have an individual feeling, as in this humorous picture of Pisa, right. *Pentax, 35 mm, Ektachrome 64, 1/250, f8.*

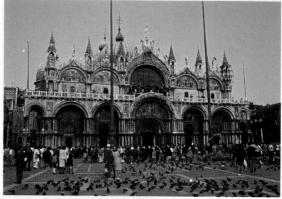

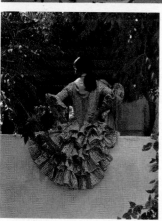

▲ **Don't avoid the obvious angle** just for the sake of it; the view of St Mark's in Venice, above, is taken from a picture postcard point of view, but using a wide-angle lens has given greater depth to the picture, suggesting the bustling atmosphere of a busy city. *Pentax, 28 mm, Kodachrome II, 1/30, f11.*

◀ **An untypical view** of a typical Spanish dress. I photographed this girl as she was waiting to take part in the parade at the annual sherry festival in Jerez. It is not easy to see the shape of the dress with the dancer in motion, but this casual pose captures its form perfectly. *Leicaflex, 90 mm, Ektachrome 64, 1/250, f8.*

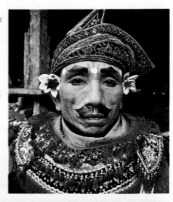

▶ **Close-ups** of people can successfully convey the atmosphere of a foreign country. You will find that most people are not too reluctant to have pictures taken of them; however, this Balinese dancer positively welcomed the idea because he had taken a lot of time and trouble with his make-up. *Pentax, 100 mm, Ektachrome 64, 1/125, f8.*

▼ **Shooting from unusual positions** is often effective—don't be put off by the amused reactions of onlookers if you need to lie flat on your stomach as I did to take this Sri-Lankan dancer. *Contax, 50 mm, Ektachrome 64, 1/250, f11.*

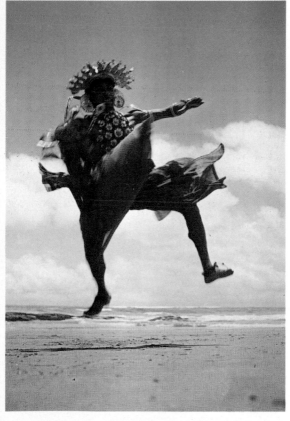

Holidays

Holiday pictures should record all the spontaneous fun of the event, becoming lively snapshots. Try to have your camera with you at all times so that you do not miss the right moment and so your companions get used to you · photographing them. You will not always be able to get uncluttered backgrounds so remember that a low camera angle can often minimize problem backgrounds, as in the picture of the girl balancing on the beach ball, right. It has also made her achievement seem the greater.

▶ *Minolta, 55 mm, Ektachrome 64, 1/125, f8.*

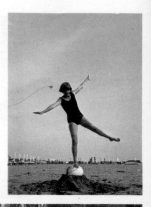

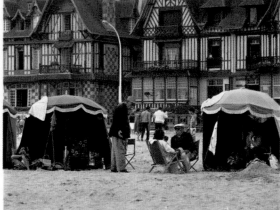

▲ **Use a long lens** to capture local scenes such as the spirited conversation between two families on the beach at Deauville, above. By taking the picture in this way I was able to emphasize the setting and to catch the people at an unguarded moment. *Pentax, 100 mm, Ektachrome 64, 1/125, f8.*

▶ **Add interest** to pictures of children by capturing some background detail. The boat behind the child, right, is in fact being sailed by his brother. I might have used a long lens to close up the two images, but as I only had a fixed-lens camera to hand I made the best of the composition by placing the boy in the foreground so the sea linked the images. *Vivitar 35EF, automatic, Ektachrome 64.*

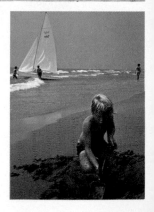

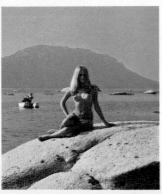

Strong sunlight is not ideal for most pictures but it can be made to work for you. In the classic holiday pose, left, I made sure the light was coming from the side to give good modelling to the girl's body and left her face in the shadow so she could look straight out without squinting. The light rock reflected light in shadow areas. I had to photograph the girl below when the light was in the wrong position. In such cases it is always better to capture the cheerful atmosphere than to worry about slight faults in technique.

◀ *Practika, 50 mm, Agfachrome 50S, 1/500, f5.6.*
▼ *Vivitar 35EF, Ektachrome 64.*

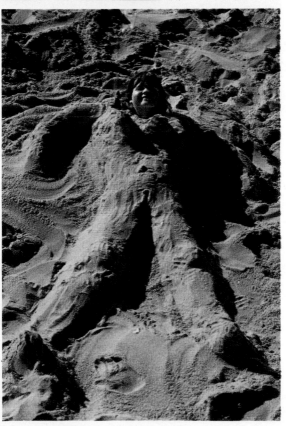

Seaside

Seaside pictures are usually taken when you are on holiday. Make the most of this opportunity to take photographs that are more than just holiday snapshots. Observe your surroundings; watch the changing light, the movement of the water, reflections and the effect of weather conditions in general. Keep your camera ready at all times to capture the unusual and unexpected.

▶ **Not an obvious holiday shot**, this silhouette of a girl on the beach makes an interesting portrait. The girl's stance, the strength of the shapes and the subtle range of sunset colours reflected in the wet sand combine to evoke a powerful atmosphere. *Pentax, 100 mm, Ektachrome 200, 1/30, f4, with tripod.*

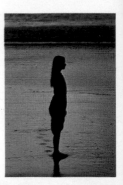

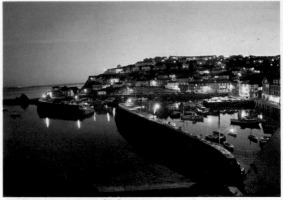

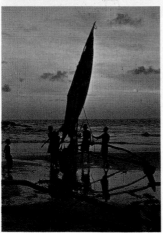

▲ **Dusk** is an excellent time to take photographs; use daylight or artificial light film according to which light predominates. Select your viewpoint so as not to leave whole areas in darkness and include some areas artificially lit to give a warm atmosphere. For long exposures of stationary objects rest your camera on a wall as I did to photograph this fishing village. *Pentax, 28 mm, Ektachrome 200 (daylight), 5 sec., f6.3.*

◀ **Take sunset shots** about a quarter of an hour after the sun has disappeared, when the sky is at its most brilliant. At this time you will be able to pick up detail in the shadows. Expose for a combination of highlight and shadow. *Rolleiflex, 55 mm, Ektachrome 64, 1/125, f8.*

▶ **For water sports** use a long lens, pre-focus and wait until the peak of the action. The surfer was taken hand-held at sufficiently fast speed to stop camera movement and arrest the action. *Pentax, 200 mm, Ektachrome 64, 1/500, f8.*

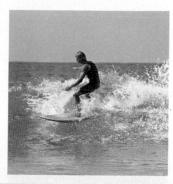

▼ **After a light shower**, these wooden breakwaters reflected the colouring of the sky and water. Shooting from the dark to the light increased the feeling of distance in this composition. None the less there is still a seaside atmosphere. *Vivitar 35EF, automatic, Ektachrome 64.*

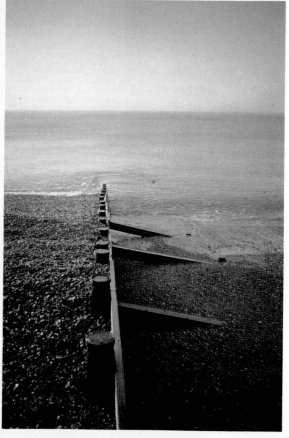

Nature and landscape

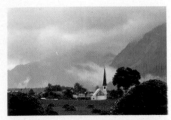

◀ **Landscape compositions** need a focal point and a sense of perspective. Here the eye is drawn into the picture by the scale of the haystacks, upwards by the church spire and across the landscape by the strong horizontal lines. Note the "aerial perspective" —where colour diminishes as background recedes. *Pentax, 28 mm, Ektachrome 200, 1/250, f8.*

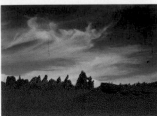

◀ **Defying the conventions** of landscape photography, this photograph of barren territory in Western Australia shows off the weird shapes of the eroded earth and the extraordinary way in which the sky echoes them. I avoided introducing a dominant subject for this reason. *Leicaflex, 21 mm, Ektachrome 64, 1/1000, f8.*

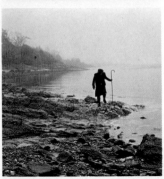

◀ **Backgrounds** like the lakeside, left, are ideal as they are rich in colour, shape and atmosphere and not overimposing. Here the central figure dominates and lends scale to the landscape. *Leicaflex, 90 mm, Ektachrome 200, 1/1000, f8.*

▼ **An aerial view** of English countryside where shadows cast by the setting sun are the strongest images. Polarizing filters help cut down reflection when shooting through Perspex windows, but simply holding a dark jacket behind your head absorbs a lot of reflection. *Minolta, 55 mm, Ektachrome 64, 1/250, f8.*

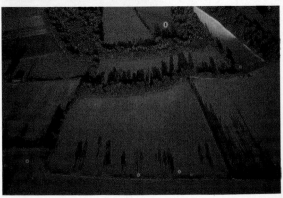

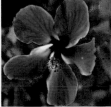

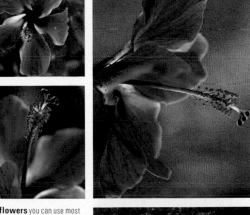

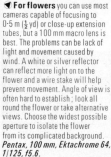

◀ **For flowers** you can use most cameras capable of focusing to 0·5 m (½ yd) or close-up extension tubes, but a 100 mm macro lens is best. The problems can be lack of light and movement caused by wind. A white or silver reflector can reflect more light on to the flower and a wire stake will help prevent movement. Angle of view is often hard to establish; look all round the flower or take alternative views. Choose the widest possible aperture to isolate the flower from its complicated background. *Pentax, 100 mm, Ektachrome 64, 1/125, f5.6.*

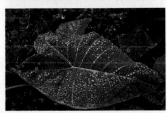

▼ **Formal subjects,** such as this Italian garden, below, need treating in a precise and straightforward way. An extreme wide-angle lens emphasizes scale and perspective. An overcast day has brought out the intensity in the greens. *Pentax, 15 mm, Ektachrome 200, 1/250, f8.*

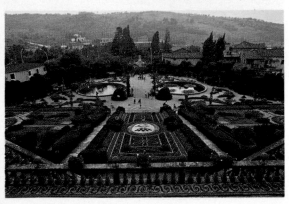

Water and underwater

You can buy elaborate equipment for underwater photography, but it is possible to achieve spectacular effects by just using an underwater camera such as a Nikonos in existing light. Waterproof cases for ordinary cameras are available, but since salt water will ruin your camera it is obviously wise to invest in the best possible protection; these cases are really only for shallow-water photography. It is best to use a wide-angle lens underwater as the angle of view is reduced by the refractive effect of water, and you can minimize this effect by getting closer to your subject. For the brightest light and the most interesting scenes you need tropical waters; in other climates flash is essential below about 5 m (15 ft).

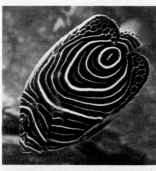

◀ **Practise focusing** and exposure by going to a diving school or a place where fish are fed regularly and are used to the proximity of humans. *Nikonos, 35 mm, Ektachrome 200, electronic flash, 1/30, f16.*

▼ **Remember that the seashore**, such as this area of the Barrier Reef with its coral and rockpools, can yield hundreds of exciting subjects for photography with an ordinary camera (but interchangeable lenses are a must). *Pentax, 50 mm, 1/500, UV filter.*

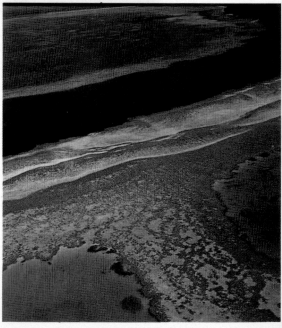

▶ Reflected in the water the brightly painted boats, right, offer an ever-changing abstract composition. Moving water is always interesting whether you take it on its own with strong reflections or introduce other subjects. *Pentax, 100 mm, Ektachrome 64, 1/250, f11.*

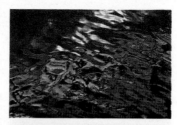

▶ Silhouette reflections of reeds taken against the light make an interesting pattern and describe the surface and quality of the water. Good reflections are seen in the early morning and evening when the sun is low and the water still. For rich colour underexpose $\frac{1}{2}$-1 stop on slide film. *Pentax, 100 mm, Ektachrome 64, 1/250, f11.*

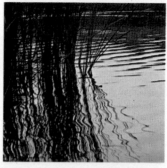

▼ To arrest the movement of the water and still capture the energetic action of the boys swimming, I used a medium-fast shutter speed. Note how the quality of water can vary in one small area. *Pentax, 100 mm, Ektachrome 64, 1/125, f8.*

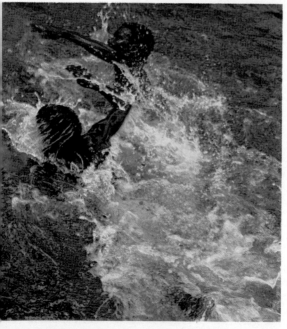

Animals in the wild

You need patience and a lot of understanding to photograph animals successfully in their natural surroundings. Get information from experts if necessary. You may need to build a hide or shoot from a car or a tent. Remote-control cameras, long lenses and tripods are all invaluable. Try to position yourself so you get an uncluttered background; failing this use selective focusing. Make use of available light as supplementary lighting is usually difficult.

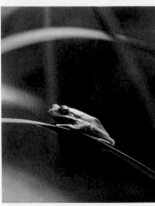

◀ **Small, fast-moving creatures** like this tree frog need a photographer who works quickly. Shooting at open aperture diffuses the background and isolates the image. I focused by moving the camera. *Leicaflex, 135 mm, Agfachrome 50S, 1/2000, widest aperture.*

▼ **I took two days** to photograph this fox. It often helps to put out a little food for a few days before you photograph. In this case we let out some chickens and I got my pictures, though the fox was not so lucky. For this sort of picture you must shoot at very fast speeds. *Minolta, 55 mm, Ektachrome 200, 1/500, f11.*

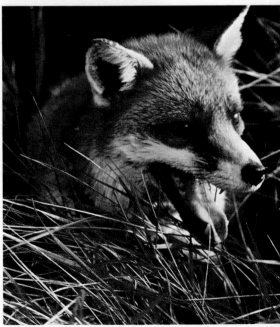

▶ **The seagull,** right, was photographed from a boat. Because both boat and bird were travelling in the same direction at a similar speed, and the bird was gliding on the wind, I was able to take the picture at 1/60. The only limitation on shutter speed was the necessity of avoiding camera shake. *Leicaflex, 90 mm, Kodachrome II, 1/60, f8.*

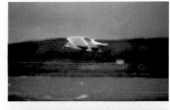

▶ **Nests** are difficult to photograph in sufficient light. Here a 100 mm macro is invaluable; open aperture and minimal depth of field are an advantage in this case as they bring out the seclusion and snugness of the nest. *Pentax, 100 mm macro, Ektachrome 200, 1/30, f4.*

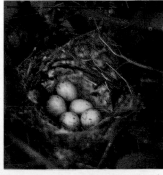

▼ **Baby birds,** such as the moorhen, below, demand extra patience. I waited 3 hours for this picture at the side of a pond; after an hour the birds felt free to come quite close to me. Continual refocusing and assessing light is necessary for this sort of shot. *Pentax, 200 mm, Ektachrome 200, 1/250, f4.*

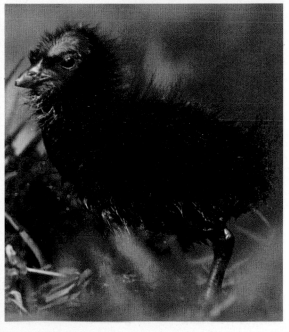

Pets and zoo animals

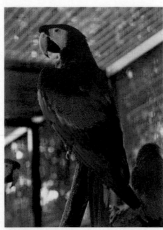

◀ **A long lens** (90 mm or longer) will enable you to eliminate wire netting or bars at the zoo. If you focus sharply on the bird or animal and then shoot at open aperture the bars will disappear, as they have in this picture of a parrot. The colour has retained its brilliance although it is slightly diffused. *Leicaflex, 135 mm, Ektachrome 64, 1/250, f 4.*

▼ **Pets,** like people, have a personality to express. Use objects familiar to them as props. Here the dog's bed both reassures him and provides an excellent colour contrast. Electronic flash is a help as it arrests movement and enables you to take pictures without problems of overheating floodlights. *Hasselblad, 150 mm, Ektachrome 64, f16, Balcar electronic flash.*

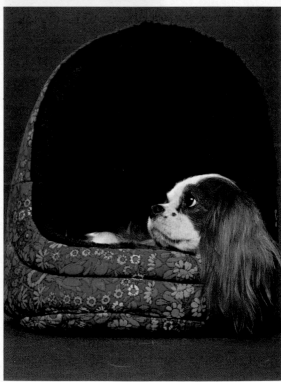

▶ **Overcast skies** can bring out a rich quality that bright sun might burn out. The pattern on this bird's wing and the overall modelling show up beautifully here. Lack of light restricted the aperture and speed, but the feeling of movement and strength is enhanced. When photographing animals you should always be alert to the possibilities of interesting and unexpected movements and be able to respond to the situation very quickly. I had already worked out the technical details of the shot when the bird suddenly spread its wings revealing a marvellously rich new area of pattern and texture. *Pentax, 50 mm, Tri-X, 1/60, f2.8.*

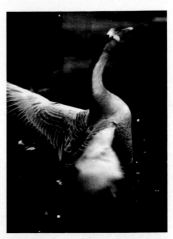

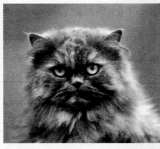

◀ **Small animals** are best photographed with SLRs, which give you ease of focusing and action—necessary with fast-moving animals.
Although this picture of a cat looks bright it was taken in subdued lighting ; this was deliberate in order to make the eyes appear brighter. *Pentax, 100 mm, Tri-X, 1/125, f4.*

▶ **Zoo animals** are often easier to photograph because they are used to people, but it can be very difficult in some zoos to get a natural-looking uncluttered background. The photographer is at the mercy of the animals and must wait until they take up the sort of pose he is looking for. These black swans were taken first thing in the morning when you can be sure there will be few people about. Notice that I positioned myself to shoot slightly against the light ; this was in order to bring out the texture of their feathers, which would otherwise have appeared solid black. *Vivitar 35EF automatic, Tri-X.*

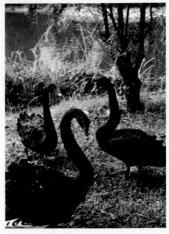

Studio techniques

Almost any combination of images can be achieved in studio conditions, often with a limited amount of equipment, and it is not hard to select certain areas and mask out others (see pp.114-15). However, simple, well-thought-out combinations are usually the most successful. As well as being fun to do these images can combine subjects you could not possibly have photographed together and they can also provide a disturbingly different view of the familiar. To photograph a model in a location that you have on slide but cannot get to, simply project the background image on to a screen, as shown right, position the model in front of it, light from one side and shoot both images together. (See details below.)

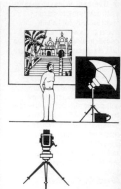

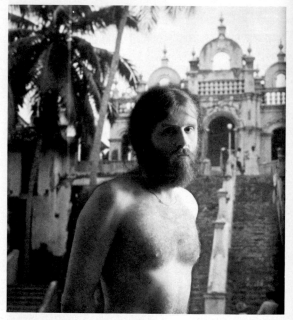

▲ **Front projection** has set the London student above in an exotic Indian location. This technique requires the image axis of the projector to be identical to the lens axis of the camera. Position the projector parallel to the screen and bounce the image off a semi-silvered mirror, set at an angle of 45°, on to it. Behind the mirror, position the camera so that its lens exactly aligns with the redirected image. Use a highly reflective, glass-beaded screen to throw back a bright image and to make any unwanted image falling on the model appear dim in comparison. Light the model separately to kill the image. If all angles are correct the model in front of the screen should always mask his or her own shadow.

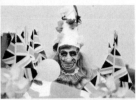

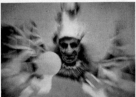

◀ **The effect of a zoom lens** can be produced in the studio. For the picture left I projected the image on to a flat white-painted wall, placed the camera with a zoom lens behind the projector and changed focal length during the exposure. As you can see it is impossible to tell that the picture was not originally shot with a zoom. *Vivitar, 70-210 mm, Tri-X, 1/4, f5.6.*

▼ **Multiple images,** such as the dramatic shot below, can be achieved by using two projectors (diagram below). I used the mouth alone as the main shot and superimposed a double exposure on it. To take the full face and profile I used a black velvet background and exposed separately for each image, lighting the face in each case from one direction only. *Hasselblad, 150 mm, Tri-X, 1/15, f8.*

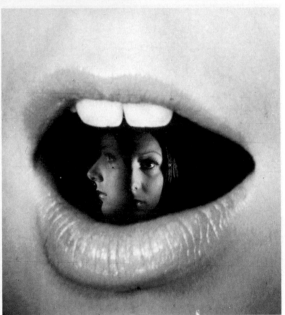

◀ **Using two projectors,** I first projected the shot of the mouth; with the other projector I positioned the double exposure of the girl's head in the darkened area in the centre of the picture and photographed the screen to get the final image. You can vary the size of the final image by moving the projectors in relation to the screen.

Studio techniques

▼ **Stroboscopic lights** can give exciting multiple images. It is usually necessary to have a black, or at any rate a dark, background so that the images show up clearly—they tend to burn out in light backgrounds. Best results are obtained when flashes are fired relatively slowly (about 10 per second) as too many superimposed images can give a muddled effect. It used to be the case that you needed a complicated set-up to achieve the right effect, but stroboscopic lamps with variable controls—up to 20 flashes per second—are now available; you can use these to give any number of flashes during an exposure and time the frequency to suit the movement you are recording. To get clearly defined images of the belly dancer below I used 5 flashes per second. *Rolleiflex, 80 mm, Tri-X, f16.*

▶ **Television or cinema screens** provide an unending source of potential images. To photograph a television screen you should use a shutter speed no faster than 1/30 because the picture on the tube is re-formed many times a second and you will need to have several scans during the exposure in order to record the complete image successfully. If using colour film it is best to choose the type balanced for daylight use. Always darken the room first in order to increase screen contrast. Never use flash as it will destroy contrast completely. Subjects such as the science-fiction character, right, are excellent for combining with other images to create unusual effects. Remember to obtain permission first if using your camera in a cinema. *Pentax, 105 mm, Tri-X, 1/15, f11.*

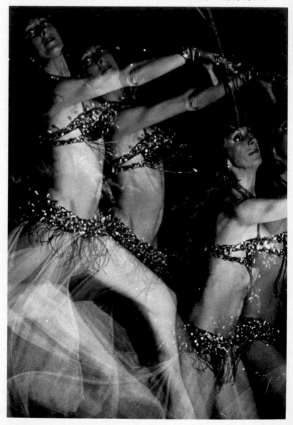

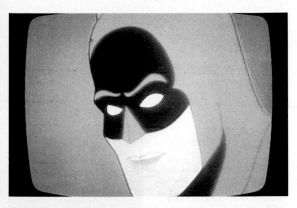

Double exposure is a camera technique that you can use if you do not have the facilities for front projection. The results are less predictable but it, too, allows you to increase or reduce the apparent size of objects by making contrasts of scale. If you are using a camera without a double exposure facility, take your first image and then tighten the film in the cassette with the rewind knob. Depress the release button on the base plate of the camera to disengage the sprockets and then wind on. This should

retension the shutter without advancing the film. In the picture below, the eye was cut out of a magazine and I photographed it with a Hasselblad and a 150 mm lens. After copying this image I marked the position of the bottom of the eyelid on the camera focusing screen. To darken it a little I underexposed half a stop. Next I posed the girl against a black velvet background, then positioned the camera so she appeared below the line in the lower half of the frame and re-exposed the frame using an 80 mm lens.

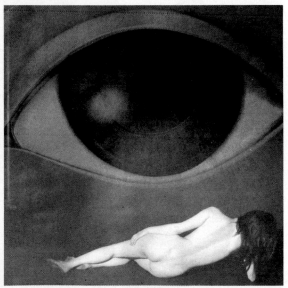

Interiors

To capture the atmosphere of an interior I prefer to use existing light, with a small flash as auxiliary lighting only if absolutely necessary. Shoot from doorways or through a window to get as much space as possible and keep the light behind you whenever you can. Remember snow is an excellent natural source of extra light as it bounces light up, making dark ceilings visible.

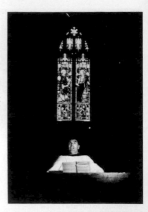

▶ **Fading light** coming through a stained-glass window and a solitary spotlight on the organist created this atmosphere of an evening service. This was enhanced by the fact that there was little light in the rest of the church. *Rolleiflex, 80 mm, Tri-X, f5.6 with tripod.*

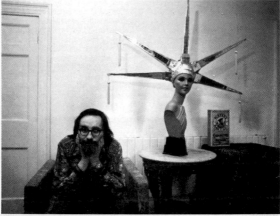

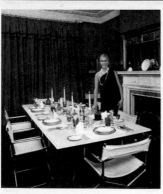

▲ **A small flash bounced off the ceiling** reinforced existing light in the rather melancholy atmosphere, above. This is a good way to increase light without destroying the mood. *Pentax, 55 mm, Pan-X, 1/60, f5.6.*

◀ **To look correct through the camera** things may have to be moved. When photographing small interiors you may have to compensate by moving furniture or other objects. What appears right in reality may look wrong from the camera's single viewpoint. For formal lighting I used two electronic flashes bounced off the white ceiling. *Hasselblad, 60 mm, Plus-X, 1/25, f16.*

▶ **Side-lighting** has brought out all the detail in the ornate temple, right. The figure of the watchful monk makes a sharp contrast with the statue and brings the picture alive. In poor light, using fast film, I was able to hand-hold the camera. *Rolleiflex, 80 mm, Tri-X, 1/60, f8.*

▼ **Large interiors** present two major problems: including enough of the subject in the picture and keeping vertical and horizontal lines parallel. To solve them you need to use a view camera with all movements or a wide-angle shift lens. The shift lens is convenient, but I prefer the view camera. *Linhof, 150 mm, Plus-X, 5 sec., f32.*

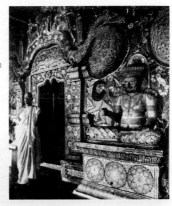

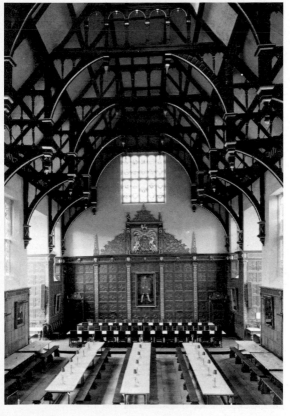

Architecture

You need to understand and appreciate different styles to photograph architecture successfully. Traditional buildings are usually best taken in a straightforward, obvious way, as the architect meant them to be seen. But remember to explore other possibilities as well: use archways and windows for framing, shoot reflections in puddles or windows, or pick a small area to represent the whole.

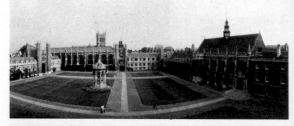

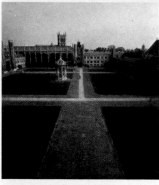

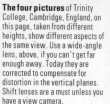

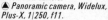

The four pictures of Trinity College, Cambridge, England, on this page, taken from different heights, show different aspects of the same view. Use a wide-angle lens, above, if you can't get far enough away. Today they are corrected to compensate for distortion in the vertical planes. Shift lenses are a must unless you have a view camera.
▲ *Panoramic camera, Widelux, Plus-X, 1/250, f11.*
◀ The view of the college, left, was taken from the roof of the Gatehouse ; the height provides a pleasing perspective. Try to get an unobtrusive figure in the picture to give a sense of scale.

◀ Taken from the same height but as a horizontal composition, this view is a little easier on the eye than the more imposing composition above. Patterns made by the paths are less obtrusive but serve the same purpose of leading the eye to the main subject of the picture.

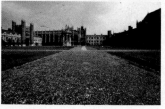

◀ From ground level, although the paths dominate the composition, the buildings look more substantial. The lower view, because it is the one most commonly seen, is more intimate and more involved. By the angle and shape you choose you can make different areas more significant. Here the path is prominent ; the vertical lines take the eye into the picture and the horizontal ones draw the eye across. *(All pictures) Pentax, 15 mm, Plus-X, 1/250, f11.*

▶ **Details** of old buildings can reveal superb craftsmanship; don't overlook them. I used a red filter to bring out the grain in the wood of the door panel, right. The direction of the light has emphasized the modelling. Use long lenses for high, inaccessible places — a 100 mm or even a 200 mm is useful. If possible use a tripod so you don't have to worry about movement. *Vivitar 35EF automatic, Plus-X.*

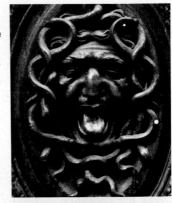

▼ **Capture the flavour** of a whole building simply by photographing a detail. The section of the timbered building, below, reveals a lot about the architecture while it forms a segment of pattern and an interesting composition. *Hasselblad, 60 mm, Plus-X, ½ sec., f16.*

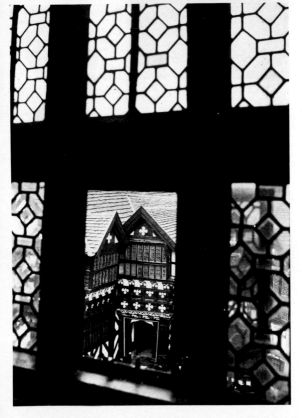

Architecture

Modern architecture is characterized by its stark simplicity,
its use of line and space and lack of ornamental detail;
consequently it is very effective to photograph modern
buildings in a graphic way. Look for road signs and other
examples of contemporary design to emphasize this quality and,
where you are photographing a building with a lot of glass,
wait for light to give interesting effects.

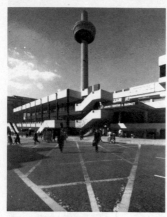

◀ **To attract the eye** and lead
it to the tower I included the
lines on the ground in the
composition, left. I used a shift
lens, which means you can raise
the viewpoint and the verticals are
corrected; it will give a slight
fall-off at the top of the picture—
this is usually sky, which will be
darkened slightly. *Pentax, 28 mm
shift lens, Agfachrome 50S,
1/250, f8.*

▼ **Side-light** on the modern
library has given it the appearance
of a silhouette, showing the
strength and solidity of this
predominantly glass building. The
figures lend a sense of scale and
a touch of humanity. *Rollei,
80 mm, 1/250, f8.*

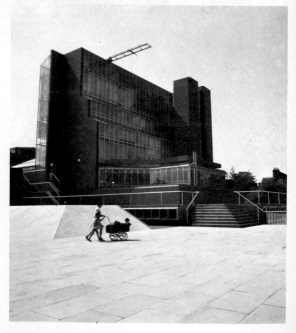

▶ **By framing a building**, as in the picture of Sydney Opera House, right, taken behind a breakwater, you get a sense of distance and you also link the building with the foreground: this is a useful professional trick which often produces a more interesting and unusual picture. Look out for conveniently situated arches, doorways or windows—or shoot through an old film box.
Vivitar 35EF, automatic.

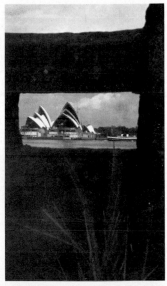

▼ **To bring out relief** in this detail of the cathedral in Liverpool I used strong side-lighting; to give greater contrast I underexposed one stop. Notice also the quality of the detail in the stonework. Although it is a good idea to include figures to give scale make sure they look fairly anonymous and do not dominate the picture. If you want to remove figures, provided they are moving and not in strong light, use slow film and a long exposure. *Pentax, 28 mm, 1/250, f16.*

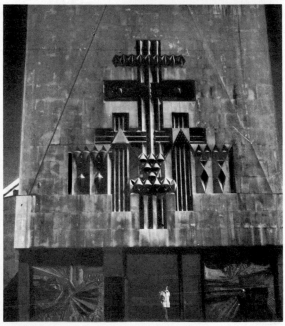

The darkroom/Layout and equipment

For home processing and printing you do not need a permanent darkroom. A bathroom makes an ideal temporary darkroom as water is readily available. Other essential requirements are access to a power supply to run the enlarger and safelights, the ability to make the room light-tight to avoid fogging light-sensitive film and papers and, finally, some form of ventilation. For ease of use and to avoid splashing negatives and paper with chemicals, your darkroom should be divided into two areas—a dry bench and a wet bench.

The dry bench area of your darkroom should include, as a minimum, an enlarger and lens, print easel, focusing magnifier and an accurate second timer. Even if your budget is limited it is best not to skimp on the enlarger lens. There is little point in spending a lot of money on a camera lens if your enlarger lens is not capable of producing a satisfactorily sharp photograph. Dodgers and burners (see p. 115) can be made for virtually no expense and allow you control over selected areas of a print. Print trimmers, print dryers, spare negative carriers, a small desk light box for examining slides and negatives and a selection of different surfaces and grades of printing papers can all be added as your technique becomes more sophisticated.

 1 Print trimmer
 2 Ruler
 3 Scalpel
 4 Tape dispenser
 5 Timer
 6 Scissors
 7 Dodgers
 8 Safelight
 9 Print easel
10 Focus magnifier
11 Enlarger
12 Wall clock
13 Burner
14 Storage area

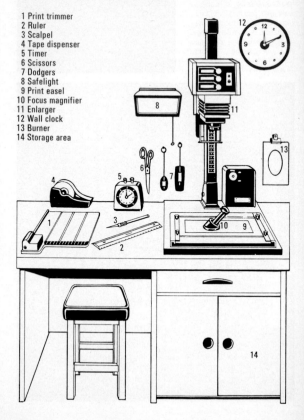

The wet bench area of your darkroom should include all the equipment and accessories you will need for processes involving water or chemicals. It is worth remembering that a lot of the time you will be working in total darkness, if processing films or printing with paper designed for colour photography, or in a dim orange or red light, if using paper for black and white photography, so it is best to adopt a very methodical approach to darkroom layout. Many rolls of film and prints will be saved if bottles of dilute chemicals, trays, timers and print tongs are always placed in the same position on shelves or on the work surfaces and conveniently to hand.

Print processing trays should be laid out in the order they are needed—developing tray, stop bath and fixer. If water is available in the darkroom the fixer tray is best positioned next to the water supply. Two different types of print washer are available—a high-capacity vertical washer and a low-capacity, cheaper, horizontal washer. Use different coloured print tongs for each chemical process. This ensures that there will be no chemical residue carried through to the next tray to cause contamination and a shorter working capacity. To save chemicals always match tray size to paper size.

1 Developer
2 Stop bath
3 Fixer
4 Print
5 Thermometer
6 Paper towels
7 Squeegee

8 Print tongs
9 Process chemicals
10 Developing tank
11 Spiral
12 Spare trays
13 Squeegee
14 Sponge

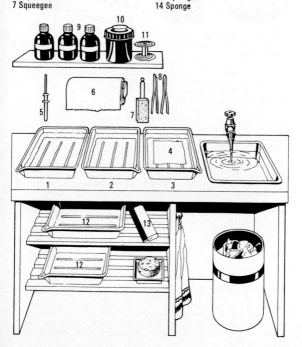

Developing black and white film

Black and white film can be processed at home in a very basic darkroom; a blacked-out bathroom or toilet will do nicely. Read the accompanying manufacturer's instructions carefully with regard to dilution, time and temperature of the process chemicals. Although some chemicals can be used more than once do not try to save money by using them more than the recommended times. Mark the bottles to indicate the number of times used.

Equipment list
Measuring jug
Developing tank
Spiral
Clips
Processing chemicals
Thermometer
Eye-dropper
Scissors
Timer
Warming bath

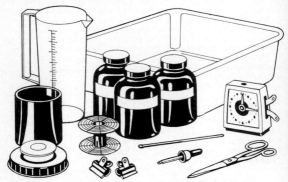

After ensuring the process chemicals are at the correct temperatures (**1**), remove the film from its cartridge or cassette in total darkness as film is panchromatic (sensitive to light of all colours). Before loading the film into the spiral of your developing tank, cut the end of the tapered leader square (**2**). Developing tanks are available in plastic or stainless steel—the latter costs more but will last a lifetime. Development commences as soon as the chemical comes in contact with the emulsion, so try and pour the developer in quickly (**3**). At the end of each cycle ensure the chemical is drained quickly as well because chemical reaction continues until the tank is empty of solution. Once the film is completely covered by solution it will need to be agitated to ensure all the emulsion is in constant contact with fresh solution (**4**). When the stop and fixing processes are complete (**5** and **6**) a wetting agent can be introduced to the tank after the film is washed. This wetting agent allows the film to dry evenly, so eliminating drying marks on the emulsion. The most efficient washing technique is accomplished by inserting a rubber tube into the centre of the tank top and turning on the tap. Water filters are available to remove the tiny particles of grit from tap water that might damage the emulsion (**7**). After a thorough wash the film can be hung in a dust-free environment until dry or placed in a heated film-drying cabinet (**8**).

Reversal film often needs to be re-exposed to light before the colour developer stage. The partially processed film must be removed from the spiral and evenly exposed on both sides approximately 30 cm (2 ft) from a Number 2 photoflood bulb.

After all processing is complete and the film is dry, cut negatives into conveniently sized strips (not single negatives) and store them in specially designed acid-free paper sleeves. Slides can, of course, be cut into single frames, mounted and stored. (For details on storing negatives and slides, see pp. 26-7.)

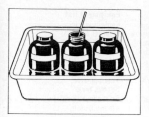

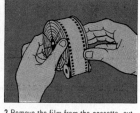

1 Bring all chemicals to the correct temperature, 20°C (68°F), by standing them in a dish of warm water. As the temperature drops, top up with hot water.

2 Remove the film from the cassette, cut the leader square and load it on to the spiral, making sure it loads evenly to prevent the film buckling.

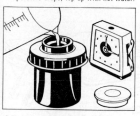

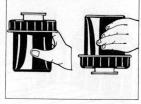

3 Place loaded spiral in tank and pour in the developer quickly. Rap the tank on the bench to disperse any air bubbles and start timer immediately.

4 To ensure even flow of fresh solution agitate the tank for 10 seconds in each minute of recommended development. Rap tank on bench to remove air bubbles.

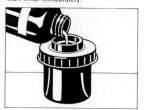

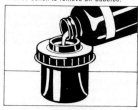

5 After removing all the developer pour in the stop bath until it overflows. Agitate the tank continuously for 10-15 seconds to neutralize any remaining developer.

6 Discard the stop bath and pour in the fixer. Fixation takes from 5 to 10 minutes and the tank needs to be agitated for 10 seconds out of every minute.

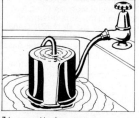

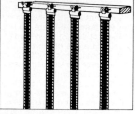

7 Insert a rubber hose down into the centre of the tank and allow a fast flow of water to wash through the film for 30 minutes. Use a filter to remove grit.

8 Hang film up to dry and attach a film clip to the bottom to prevent curling. Remove excess water by gently drawing a sponge down the film's length.

Making black and white contact prints

Contact printing your black and white films is the most economical method of deciding which negatives should be enlarged. A whole film of 36 negatives can be printed on one sheet of 20 x 25 cm (8 x 10 in) paper—producing an image size exactly the same as the negative's. Slight variations of contrast, exposure, composition and subject matter, which are not apparent when you look at the negatives, can easily be seen on the contact sheet. Once made, the contact sheet can be filed with your negatives to form a permanent record of your work.

Equipment list
Contact printer
Enlarger and lens
Printing paper
Process chemicals (developer, stop and fix)
Developing trays (3)
Thermometer
Second timer
Print tongs (2 sets)
Cleaning cloth
Cleaning fluid
Blower brush
Print washer

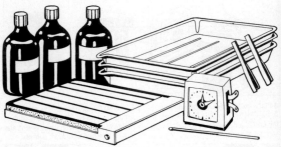

For best results, a methodical approach to darkroom work is essential. At all stages of preparation—mixing chemicals, selecting aperture and paper grade and length of exposure—make a note of any factors that might need to be duplicated at a later stage.

The first step in making a contact sheet is to mix the process chemicals—developer, stop and fix—and bring them to the correct temperature (**1**). This will vary between manufacturers, but should be about 20°C (68°F). Purpose-built contact printers are the easiest to use, but any flat, clean surface and a sheet of glass will do. If using 35 mm film, cut it into strips consisting of six negatives. For a 36-exposure film this will give you six strips—just the right number for 20 x 25 cm (8 x 10 in) paper. Open the glass lid of the contact printer and, using a lint-free cloth and cleaning fluid, remove all grease marks and dust. Using a blower brush, clean the negatives thoroughly. Load each strip of negatives into the special slots on the glass. Ensure that the negatives are loaded emulsion-side down and that the frame numbers are not obscured by the slots (**2**). Once all the strips have been loaded, turn the room lights off and position a piece of printing paper, emulsion-side up, on the base of the contact printer (**3**). Bring the glass lid of the contact printer (holding the negatives) down firmly in contact with the printing paper on the base. Place the sandwich on the base board of your enlarger and expose the paper (**4**). You could use any white light but the enlarger lamp is probably the most convenient as it is guaranteed to give the paper an even illumination. Gauging the exposure is a matter of experience, and will vary depending on the density of the negatives and the aperture of the enlarger lens, but try 10-15 seconds at f8 for a general exposure. Remove the paper and process in the normal manner (**5, 6, 7** and **8**).

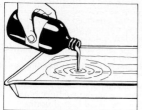

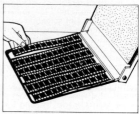

1 Bring the developer, stop and fix to the correct temperature and pour the chemicals into the developing trays.

2 Cut the negatives into strips of six and slot them, emulsion-side down, into the glass lid of the contact printer.

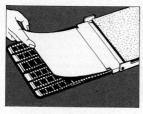

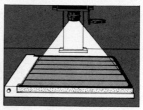

3 Place the printing paper on the base board of the contract printer. Ensure it is emulsion-side up.

4 Bring the negatives and printing paper into contact, place the contact printer on the enlarger base board and expose.

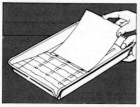

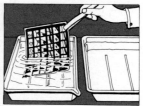

5 Tip the developer tray forward, place paper in the tray and lay it down to allow developer to wash back over paper.

6 Allow excess developer to drain back into tray before transferring paper into the stop bath.

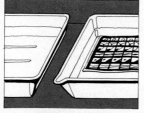

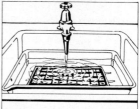

7 Using a different set of print tongs to avoid contamination of chemicals, transfer the print into the fixer.

8 When fixing is complete, wash the print thoroughly in a fast-moving supply of fresh water.

Making enlargements and print control

For the photographer working in black and white attention to detail is as important in the darkroom as it is with the camera.

The process of selection and control exercised when you decide what to photograph and how to photograph it can be given a further dimension once inside the darkroom. Having made a contact print (see pp. 112-13) and chosen the negatives you wish to enlarge, selective printing can commence.

Choose chemicals and contrast grades of paper carefully as they can be used to manipulate the purity of your whites or the densities of your blacks. Paper surface can also be used as a means of disguising an overly grainy negative or diffusing an overly sharp image. Moving the enlarger head higher up the column allows you to select which part of the original negative to record. Excessively contrasty negatives can be selectively exposed so as to hold back the blacks to stop shadow detail blocking up or to give highlights additional exposure to bring out detail that would otherwise be lost.

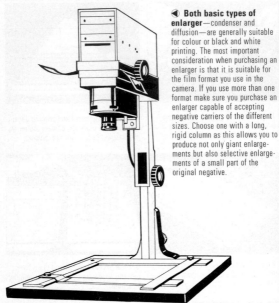

◀ **Both basic types of enlarger**—condenser and diffusion—are generally suitable for colour or black and white printing. The most important consideration when purchasing an enlarger is that it is suitable for the film format you use in the camera. If you use more than one format make sure you purchase an enlarger capable of accepting negative carriers of the different sizes. Choose one with a long, rigid column as this allows you to produce not only giant enlargements but also selective enlargements of a small part of the original negative.

Black and white printing allows you a choice of contrast grades varying from 0 (very soft) to 6 (very hard). Negatives lacking in contrast might benefit from being printed on grades 3, 4 or 5, whereas a contrasty negative might be better printed on grades 0, 1 or 2. Grade 6 will eliminate nearly all shades of grey.

Once you have decided which negative to print, inspect it carefully for drying marks, abrasions or dust. Dust can be removed using a blower brush or anti-static cloth or gun. Drying marks may necessitate rewashing and drying the film, prints made from scratched negatives will need retouching.

Equipment list
Process chemicals
Printing paper
Enlarger and lens
Blower brush
Anti-static gun or cloth
Print easel
Timer
Different sized dodgers
Rigid wire
Black tape
Different sized burners

▶ **Making a test strip** allows you to look at three controlled exposures on the same sheet of printing paper and to assess which is best suited to the print. Place the negative in the negative carrier and project the image on to the print easel. Judge which part of the image contains the most representative tones, turn the enlarger off and place the test strip across that area. Next, turn on the enlarger and give the whole strip 10 seconds exposure. After this initial exposure, shield one-third of the strip with a piece of card and continue the exposure for another 10 seconds. Then position the card so that it covers two-thirds of the strip and give it a further 10 seconds.

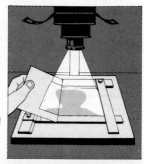

▶ **Clean off fingerprints or dust** before loading the negative into the carrier. Inspect the enlarger lens as well. Then, with the room lights off, project the negative on to the print easel with the lens aperture wide open, adjust the height of the enlarger head to control the degree of enlargement and focus the image. Turn off the enlarger, place a sheet of printing paper in the easel and close the aperture down to the f-stop used to make the test strip (f8 or f11 is best). As you turn on the enlarger again, start the timer and expose the paper for the length of time indicated by the test strip.

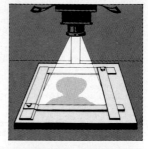

▶ **Dodging** is a darkroom technique used to hold light away from selected areas of the print which might otherwise print too dark. A dodger can be made from any piece of non-reflective, preferably black, card. Shape the dodger to approximately the size of the area you want to mask and attach it to a long piece of rigid wire. To stop the wire from reflecting unwanted light on to the print, cover it with black insulating tape. When using the dodger, keep it continually on the move, otherwise a clearly defined area of lighter tone will be evident. More than one dodger can be used to cover different areas of the print.

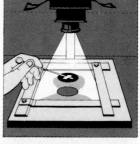

▶ **Burning-in** is the opposite of dodging. Take a piece of non-reflecting card large enough to cover the printing paper being used. Into this card cut an aperture (or apertures) corresponding to the areas (probably highlights) of the print you want to receive more exposure. When most of the print has received sufficient exposure, cover the print with the card, allowing only the selected areas of the print to receive additional light. This technique can be extended to allow you to print vignettes around the edges of your prints. Keep the card moving to soften the lines round the area being burnt in.

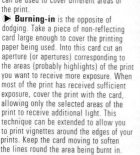
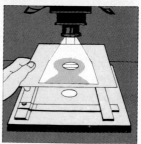

Developing colour film

Slide film is probably the most immediately satisfying to process, since the slides can be put into mounts and projected as soon as they are dry. Colour processing is more involved than black and white processing as it uses more individual chemical bath steps, and accurate maintenance of the high solution temperatures is of utmost importance. The chemicals will vary depending on the film to be developed. Besides the chemicals, you will need a measuring jug, beaker and storage bottle for each solution, each of which should be clearly marked and not contaminated with any other solution thereafter. You will also need a very good colour-processing thermometer, preferably scaled in increments of 0.25°C. Some colour-processing chemicals can be harmful if used without caution; wear a protective apron and rubber gloves. A single film may be developed in an enclosed tank, but two or more may be more easily developed in total darkness using a tall open-topped tank and the dunking method. This requires a processing timer with a luminous dial which can be used in the dark.

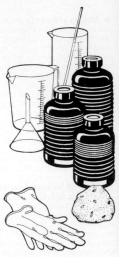

Aids for mixing working-strength solutions from the concentrate are simply the measuring beakers and a stirring stick. Be careful not to splash any of the solutions on your clothing.

Colour negative films

Virtually all colour negative films can be home processed, but the most common process is called C-41. Processing is not complicated and results are good providing you follow the manufacturer's directions carefully. The seven commonly found steps, their times and temperatures are: colour developer, $3\frac{1}{4}$ min, 37.8°C; bleach, $6\frac{1}{2}$ min, 24°C; wash, $3\frac{1}{4}$ min, 38°C; fix, $6\frac{1}{2}$ min, 24°C; wash, $3\frac{1}{4}$ min, 38°C; stabilize, $1\frac{1}{2}$ min, 24°C; and dry (time and temperature variable).

Colour slide films

Most colour slide films can be easily home processed, but non-substantive films such as Kodachrome and Anscochrome cannot since the dye couplers responsible for the final colour image are in the manufacturer's process chemicals. Substantive colour slide films have the dye couplers incorporated in the emulsion. Make certain you purchase the correct chemical kit for the film you are to develop (see p.130)—they do vary. Although most processes require a high temperature, 3M and other companies now manufacture a kit that works at the usual black and white processing temperatures of 20°C (68°F), which is easier to obtain and maintain. Slide films need to be fogged (re-exposed to white light) partway through processing to reverse the image from a negative to a positive one. Depending on the kit, this may also be done chemically.

Chemical activity

The factors governing chemical activity are the same as those in black and white processing—time and temperature. However, as there is less margin for error in colour film processing, the times and temperatures recommended in each chemical kit must be rigidly adhered to.

In addition to working accurately, you must also work quickly. The first colour-developer time in the C-41 process is only $3\frac{1}{4}$ min compared to, say, 6-12 min for a black and white film. Therefore, tank draining and refilling times must be kept to the absolute minimum. This is quite easy when only one film is being developed, but if more than one is to be processed, then the dunking method is recommended. This requires a separate tank for each solution. Processing is carried out in total darkness with no lids on the tanks. At the end of each processing stage, the film is quickly pulled out of the tank, excess solution is lightly shaken off and the film is then placed in the next solution.

Essential equipment for colour-film and print processing
Processing tank(s) and spirals
Chemical-measuring beakers
Chemical-storage bottles for working-strength solutions still usable for further processing
Deep trays for tank and print-tray temperature maintenance
High-temperature colour thermometer marked in 0.25°C gradations
Rubber gloves and protective apron
Shallow print-developing trays of the required print size for economy of chemical solution
Squeegee for removing excess water from film before drying
Weighted film-hanging clips
Processing timer scaled in minutes with a sweep second hand

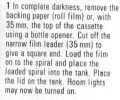

1 In complete darkness, remove the backing paper (roll film) or, with 35 mm, the top of the cassette using a bottle opener. Cut off the narrow film leader (35 mm) to give a square end. Load the film on to the spiral and place the loaded spiral into the tank. Place the lid on the tank. Room lights may now be turned on.

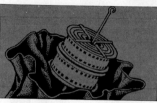

2 Mix all chemical concentrates to the correct strength. Ensure each solution is at its recommended temperature, which can be maintained by placing the beaker in a deep tray of warm water. If it is at the upper limit as processing begins, it can "drift" down to the lower limit while the processing cycle takes place.

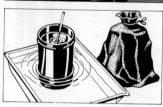

3 If developing more than one or two films at the same time, use the dunking method. You will need to have each working-strength solution in a separate tank of adequate size to cover all the films being processed. Each tank should be in a deep tray bath of warm water to ensure the correct temperature is maintained.

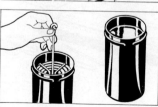

4 At each film-washing stage the film must be immersed in a constantly changing water supply. A length of hose from the tap running into the tank will do, but the water temperature should be carefully controlled, necessitating some sort of mixing tap. To remove damaging particles, a water filter should be fitted on the tap.

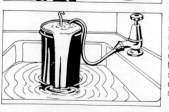

Making colour prints

Never before has it been so easy to make your own colour prints at home. With such new products as the Agfachrome-Speed paper and activator and the Kodak Ektaflex range you can make colour prints from either colour negatives or colour slides very simply and speedily. As clear, detailed instructions are supplied with these products, I shall here describe the traditional method of making colour prints.

Colour-printing equipment starts with the colour enlarger (1). It differs from the black and white model by its colour-mixing head (2) with adjustable dial-in filters of cyan, magenta and yellow. This requires a voltage stabilizer/transformer unit (3) for the 12-volt lamp inside. This heart of the system is backed up by such accessories as measuring beakers (4), trays (5), timer (6), cotton gloves (7), paper easel (8), thermometer (9) and scissors (10). The print itself is developed in a plastic drum (11), much like the tank used to develop the film.

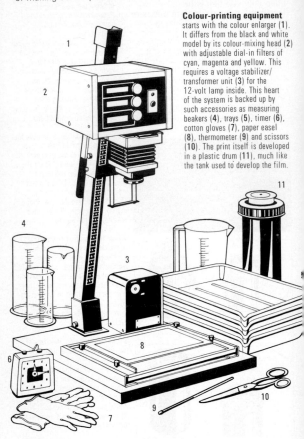

The traditional colour-print developing chemicals and colour-film developing chemicals need to be kept to very critical temperatures during each stage of the processing cycle; quite often this is to within ±0.5°C at a solution temperature of around 38°C (100°F). Therefore, the developing tank, film spiral and chemical beakers should be pre-heated with warm water prior to use. The tank and trays can then be immersed in a warm-water bath during processing to maintain the correct temperature. To avoid contamination each measuring jug, beaker and storage bottle should be marked, and once used for a certain chemical it should not be used for any other.

Although there are some general-purpose developers on the market, colour-print developing chemicals are different from film chemicals. Colour prints are most often made from colour negatives, distinguished by their orange mask, but prints may also be made directly from transparencies, using a reversal paper such as the (Ciba-Geigy) Cibachrome A or (Kodak) Ektachrome 14RC paper and suitable chemicals. Whichever kit you use, for best results read the accompanying instructions carefully and follow them exactly.

The first print
Before the first print can be made, a test should be carried out to determine the correct filtration (to be set on the enlarger's colour filter dials) and exposure (both time and lens aperture). A colour test patch will help in determining how to adjust the filters for a second test if the colours in the first were not successful. An electronic colour analyser will soon pay for itself in terms of paper saved, and make colour printing easier, quicker and more predictable. Once the correct filtration has been determined, it should be noted down as the starting point for all further tests for negatives or slides processed in the same chemicals and printed on the same paper.

Safelighting
Most colour-printing papers need to be handled in total darkness. The darkroom must be completely blacked out until the paper has been exposed under the enlarger and placed in a print-developing drum and the lid firmly attached, making it light-tight. This is when tidiness and a methodical approach pay off. If you always arrange your items in the same order and in the same relative positions, it will be easier to locate them in the dark.

Prints from slides
Exposure characteristics are different for reversal printing papers. The more exposure you give the paper, the lighter the developed print will be. Normal filter corrections are also reversed for these papers, so note the directions carefully. Paper packs will give you suggested filtration starting points for your test print. Since the chemicals in their working strengths have a limited shelf or storage life, aim to process from six to ten prints in the same processing period. Ektachrome paper processing has nine steps (at 38°C/100°F) and takes about 12 minutes. Cibachrome processing has four steps (at 24°C/75°F) and also takes 12 minutes.

The print drum
To process a single print with the minimum of solution a plastic print drum is used. After the paper has been exposed under the enlarger, it is inserted into the drum, emulsion-side inwards, and the lid put on. Then with the room lights on and the chemical baths ready in their beakers at the correct temperature, processing can begin. The length of time it takes to pour in each chemical must count as part of the time allowed for each chemical process. The drum must be laid down and rolled back and forth to allow the chemical solution inside to wash back and forth over the paper. Each chemical in turn is then emptied out and replaced with the next until processing is complete. Draining time of chemicals also counts as part of the total processing time. A motorized drum base will automatically roll the drum for you, but this adds to the cost of colour printing and is by no means necessary. Durst's RCP20 is a more costly machine print processor for 20 x 25 cm (8 x 10 in) prints, but you can simply insert the exposed paper in one end and eight minutes later receive the finished print (still wet) at the other end.

Common errors

1

CAMERA CARE

Problem Developed film shows dark streaks, and prints show bright light streaks and/or rows of sprocket hole shadows.

Cause Light has reached the film before it has been exposed in the camera, or before it has been developed.

Solution Load and unload the film in a shady area, not in direct, bright sunlight. If no shade is available, simply turn your back to the sun and load or unload the film in your own shadow.

2

Problem Long scratches along the length of negatives or slides.

Cause These tracks are probably caused by dirty film guide rails or grit in the light-tight felt trap of the film cassette.

Solution Polish film guide rails with a lens cleaning cloth or lens tissue. Never remove film cassettes from their sealed containers until you are ready to load the camera.

3

Problem Torn sprocket holes.

Cause The rewind release button (often found on the base-plate of the camera) was not depressed.

Solution Ensure that the release button is fully depressed until the film has been rewound into the cassette.

4

Problem Pictures lack "bite" or sharp focus mixed with dull appearance, low in contrast or muddy looking.

Cause Front and/or rear element of the lens is dusty or has been smeared with a fingerprint.

Solution Prevention is better than cure, so if your camera is not in use keep the lens cap on. Always avoid touching the front or rear elements of your lenses, but if they do become greasy use a lens tissue or blower brush to clean the glass. Only if a lens is particularly dirty should you use a liquid lens cleaner as it can damage the delicate anti-flare coating on the glass. The ever-ready case, purchased with most cameras, is the best protection you can give your camera, shielding it from the worst effects of minor knocks, dust, rain and sea-spray. Film will not give of its best if kept, even for a short period, in very hot conditions. Remember that you should never leave a loaded camera on the rear parcel shelf of a car or in the glove box.

5

Problem Fungus (seen as slowly increasing, irregular-shaped spots) growing on the internal elements of the lens.

Cause Storing the camera in damp or humid conditions.

Solution Store your equipment in a cool, dry place and always include in your camera bag one or two packets of silica-gel to absorb any moisture. Renew or dry out the packets every few months to prevent them becoming saturated. If fungus does appear, the affected lenses must be stripped down and cleaned by a professional lens repairer.

FLASH PICTURES

6

Problem Pictures appear too light or too dark.

Cause Incorrect setting of the flashgun controls and/or not selecting the correct lens aperture for the conditions.

Solution Remember the method of deciding which aperture to use—the flashgun's guide number divided by the flash-to-subject distance equals the desired aperture. The guide number is usually printed either on the gun itself or in the handbook that accompanies it—the guide number changing depending on the ISO speed of the film used. The guide number is given as a figure either in feet or metres, so while doing the former calculation use distance measurements of the same unit. Also remember to check that the ISO speed of the film being used is set on the flashgun's controls.

7

Problem Only part of the picture is correctly exposed. One or both (opposing) edges are very dark.

Cause A camera fitted with a focal plane shutter was set at a shutter speed that was too fast to synchronize with electronic flash. When the flash was fired the shutter was only partially open, causing part of the frame to be unexposed.

Solution Check the camera's handbook to find the fastest shutter speed (called usually the X-sync speed) that can be used with electronic flash. This is normally 1/60 for horizontally travelling focal plane shutters and 1/125 for vertically travelling focal plane shutters.

8

Problem The picture is correctly exposed at the centre of the frame but becomes progressively darker towards the edges of the frame.

Cause The angle of view of the lens is wider than the spread of light coming from the flashgun.

Solution Attach a wide-angle diffuser to the flash head or bounce the flash from a reflective surface. Remember that both these solutions will cause a fall-off in the intensity of the light and the aperture will need to be opened to compensate. Knowing how much to open up is basically trial and error, so it is best to shoot a test film, bracketing exposures. The alternative, requiring no additional exposure compensation, is to use a lens with a narrower angle of view.

9

Problem People in the picture appear to have red eyes.

Cause The flash has been fired from a position too close to the lens axis. The red colour is actually a reflection from blood vessels in the back of the eye.

Solution Bounce the light off the ceiling or wall (if using colour film you need a white surface to avoid colour cast). A larger aperture will be needed to compensate for the increased flash-to-subject distance and the light lost by absorption and scattering. Another solution is to connect the flash unit to the camera using an extension lead. Supporting the camera in one hand while holding the flash above the camera in the other will remove the flash far enough from the lens axis to avoid red-eye.

10

Problem Very bright white spots (hot spots) on shiny surfaces such as mirrors, windows or shiny glazed tiles in the picture area.

Cause Light has been reflected from these surfaces straight back into the camera lens.

Solution Stand at an angle to these shiny surfaces so that the flash will reflect away from the camera lens, or use a flash umbrella or white wall to diffuse the light.

11

Problem Although the flash controls and camera aperture are set correctly the picture is overexposed or underexposed.

Cause Flash exposure is calculated assuming a certain level of reflective surfaces. If the flash is fired too near a white or lightly coloured surface too much light will be reflected back into the lens and on to the film; if near a black surface light will be absorbed.

Solution Close the lens aperture one-half to one full f stop to restrict the amount of light entering the lens; alternatively, open up one-half stop.

12

FRAMING ERRORS
Problem The tops of subjects' heads do not appear in the image area.

Cause Camera incorrectly aimed at the subject.

Solution Be careful to notice not just what the subject is doing but also ensure that all of the subject is included in the viewfinder frame. You may be too close to the subject (with a rangefinder camera) without noticing that the subject is outside the mark that indicates the area of parallax error (usually a bright-line frame within the viewfinder).

13

Problem Close-up pictures of faces in which the face appears to be slightly stretched.

Cause When a lens is used very close to a subject it tends to stretch the image towards the edges of the frame. This is somewhat evident with standard (normal) lenses, but even more so with wide-angle lenses. Facial features nearer the lens (nose and lips) appear larger than features farther away (forehead and ears).

Solution Do not stand so close to the subject that this effect is noticed in the viewfinder—usually 1.5–2 m ($1\frac{1}{2}$–2 yd) with a standard lens. If you shoot a lot of full-face portraits and your camera accepts alternative lenses, a lens in the range 80 mm to 135 mm is ideal, as it allows a single face to fill the frame without causing any distortion associated with a lens of lesser focal length.

14

Problem Extra or unwanted detail of the scene shows up in the picture, which you did not notice when you took the picture.

Cause Not paying sufficient attention to all the elements in the viewfinder and not concentrating sufficiently on composition.

Solution When taking a picture—landscape, portrait or any other scene—look not only at the main subject but at everything within the frame. You will begin to notice small details that you do not want to include. Shoot from a different angle to avoid including them in the image area. Watch for distracting telephone poles, dustbins, electric wires, etc., for these are such a common part of the scene that they are easy to overlook.

15

Problem The main subject in the picture is too small to be recognizable.

Cause The subject was not close enough to the camera.

Solution Use a longer focal length lens if your camera accepts alternative lenses, but if your camera is of the fixed-lens type you must adopt a position nearer the subject.

16

Problem A telephone pole has sprouted from your subject's head, or a tree branch appears to be growing from your subject's ear.

Cause Not paying sufficient attention to all the information in the viewfinder before the picture was taken.

Solution Pay attention to all of the scene as it appears in the viewfinder before you press the shutter release. Watch both the foreground and background, as most framing errors can be avoided by choosing a camera position carefully.

17

OTHER ERRORS
Problem Picture too light or too dark because of a seemingly incorrect daylight exposure.

Cause A number of factors could account for this. 1 The correct film speed (its ISO number) was not set on the camera. 2 The sun or other bright light was in the viewfinder frame causing the camera's exposure meter to indicate an under-exposure. 3 The metered exposure reading was taken from the wrong part of the scene.

Solution 1 Set the correct ISO factor on the camera's film speed dial. 2 Exclude the sun or other bright light from the viewfinder before you take an exposure reading. 3 Use the light meter to assess the correct exposure from the most important element in the scene.

18

Problem Pictures appear fuzzy and indistinct.

Cause Incorrect focusing.

Solution Focus carefully on the most important part of the scene. When shooting portraits, focus on the sitter's eyes or the eye closest to the camera if the sitter is not facing the camera squarely. It is very disconcerting to see a portrait if the eyes are not rendered sharply in focus, as it is the eyes that most people look at first.

19

Problem Although accurately focused, pictures still appear fuzzy and indistinct.

Cause The shutter speed was too slow for successful hand-held exposure, resulting in camera shake.

Solution Select a shutter speed suitable for the weight of the camera and lens being used. With a standard lens and camera combination a tripod, or other camera support, should be used for shutter speeds slower than about 1/60.

20

Problem Developed film is blank and unexposed.

Cause Sprocket holes in the film have not engaged with the take-up spool of the camera and the film has not been transported through the camera.

Solution When loading film into the camera ensure that the sprocket holes properly engage with the take-up spool, both top and bottom. To check if the film is winding on, look to see if the rewind crank turns when the film advance lever is operated. Also, if the film has been correctly loaded the film advance lever should feel slightly stiff when stroked.

21

Problem Developed film is blank or the image is partially obscured.

Cause With rangefinder or TLR cameras this is probably caused by forgetting to remove the lens cap or allowing fingers or part of the camera's ever-ready case to stray in front of the lens. This will not be noticed in the viewfinder as it does not show the scene as taken in by the lens—only an approximation of it. This problem does not occur with SLR cameras as the viewfinder shows exactly the scene as taken in by the lens.

Solution Always check that the lens cap has been removed before the exposure is made and that fingers and the ever-ready case are well away from the camera lens.

22

Problem Buildings shot from ground level appear to taper to a point at the top of the picture (converging verticals).

Cause The camera was pointed upwards to include the top of the building. This has emphasized the perspective, which makes parallel lines appear to come together in the distance. A common example of this is railway lines converging as they recede from the viewer. The brain largely compensates for this trick of perspective, but the camera cannot make such allowances and faithfully records the apparent distortion.

Solution Either emphasize the effect dramatically so that it does not look like a mistake, or forego including the tops of buildings. Another alternative is to use a wide-angle shift lens. The shift facility on these rather specialized lenses allows part of the lens to be raised slightly and has the same effect of eliminating the tapering as that achieved by the rising front facility of a view camera.

23

Problem It is not clear what constitutes the main subject as it is lost in a confusing foreground or background.

Cause Too small an aperture was selected, resulting in too great a depth of field. The result is that the subject, foreground and background are all in sharp focus.

Solution Choose a relatively wide aperture (and a correspondingly faster shutter speed) to yield a limited depth of field. If the main subject is the only element in the picture in sharp focus it will be given much greater emphasis. It is still important to include both foreground and background detail in order to place the subject or frame it, but it should be either rendered out of focus or made tonally different so as not to take attention away from the main point of interest. Setting is often critical to the success of a photograph, so if you are not happy about the foreground or background elements, particularly if they contain a distracting amount of detail, and your subject is movable, try to make the effort to find a more suitable setting.

24

Problem When using a telephoto converter pictures are underexposed.

Cause Converters, invaluable for the photographer who would not make sufficient use of an array of prime lenses, contain a series of glass elements that magnify a part of the image transmitted by the prime lens. But with the addition of these glass elements a certain amount of light does not reach the film, causing photographs to be underexposed unless you compensate for this effect.

Solution Follow the manufacturer's recommendations concerning the number of f stops the prime lens needs to be opened to correct exposure. TTL metering automatically adjusts for light lost if the convertoer accepts the prime lens's light meter coupling pin.

25

Problem A series of light hexagonal or octagonal shapes in a diagonal line across the picture.

Cause The sun or other bright light source was included in the lens's angle of view when the exposure was made. The shapes noticed are in fact a series of reflections from the lens iris. Lenses are coated to minimize this sort of flaring; the more expensive the lens the better the anti-flare coating.

Solution Unless you want to use this effect exclude the sun or source of bright light from the frame by using a lens hood on the front of the lens, or position yourself so that the source of the light does not shine directly into the camera lens.

26

Problem When using preset (non-FAD) lenses photographs are overexposed.

Cause FAD (fully automatic diaphragm) lenses automatically close down to the preselected f stop when the shutter release is triggered, although framing and exposure adjustments are made with the aperture fully open. Preset lenses, however, do not automatically close down, causing the exposure to be made with the lens wide open.

Solution Use the additional ring found on the lens barrel to close down the lens manually to the desired aperture before triggering the shutter release.

27

Problem Two images appear on the same picture.

Cause The same piece of film has been exposed twice in the camera.

Solution Most modern cameras have a double-exposure prevention device (the shutter is tensioned for the next frame only after the film has been advanced). Make sure your camera is of this type before you start taking pictures. If using a plate camera with sheet film, mark the top of the film holder "exposed" after taking the picture. Then reverse the holder and mark the other side.

Film types

Films are of three main types: to produce a colour negative (for a colour print – sometimes called a colour print film); to produce a black and white negative (for a black and white print – sometimes called a black and white print film); and to produce a transparent film positive or slide (called a colour slide film, colour reversal film or colour transparency film).

Colour film (negative or reversal) is balanced for one of two main types of light (colour temperature): daylight and/or electronic flash and/or blue flash bulb; or artificial (tungsten) light sources. Screw-on lens attachments (filters) are available to correct one type of light source for the other type of film (see p.131).

A film's sensitivity to light is expressed as its film speed rating, usually in ISO or the continental DIN numerical system. The higher the number, the more sensitive the film is to light and a correspondingly faster shutter speed or smaller aperture may be used.

An ISO 100 film is half as sensitive as an ISO 200 film and twice as sensitive as an ISO 50 film. In a given lighting condition, an ISO 50 film may require an exposure of f16, 1/60; the exposure in this situation for an ISO 100 film would be f16, 1/125 (or equivalent, such as f22, 1/60).

A size notation such as 135-36 indicates a 35mm film suitable for 36 exposures; similarly a 126-20 film is a 126 film for 20 exposures. Bulk lengths are sometimes available in certain formats for those who wish to economize and are willing to cut their own lengths of film and load them into reusable cassettes.

Popular black and white negative films

Name	ISO speed	Sizes generally available
AGFA-GEVAERT		
Agfapan APX 25	25	135-36, 120 roll
Agfapan APX 100	100	135-20/36,120 roll
Agfapan APX 400	400	135-36, 120 roll
Agfaortho 25	25	135-36, 120 roll
FUJI		
Neopan 400	400	135-24/36, bulk, 120 roll
Neopan 1600	1600	135-24/36, bulk
ILFORD		
Pan F	50	135-20/36
FP4 Plus	125	135-20/36, bulk, 120 roll
HP5 Plus	400	135-24/36, bulk, 120 roll
XP2	400	135-24/36, 120 roll
Delta	400	135-20/36
KODAK		
T-Max 100	100	135-24/36/bulk, 120 roll
T-Max 400	400	135-24/36, bulk, 120 roll
T-Max 3200	3200	135-36
Plus-X	125	135-24/36, bulk, 120 roll
Tri-X	400	135-24/36, bulk, 120 roll
Technical Pan	25	135-36, 120 roll
Recording Film	n/a	135-36
High-speed Infra-red	n/a	135-36
KONICA		
Konica Infrared IR750	750	135-24/36, 120 roll

Popular colour negative films

Nearly all colour negative film is balanced for use in daylight, although one or two professional films are now available that can be used in tungsten light. To a certain extent, colour casts caused by artificial lighting can be corrected at the printing stage.

Unlike slide or black and white film, processing is the same for all types of colour negative film. This means that film speeds are inflexible and cannot generally be "pushed" to give the benefit of extra speed. However, the Kodak Ektapress film is designed to be re-rated, and is the only colour negative film of this type.

Name	ISO speed	Sizes generally available
AGFA-GEVAERT		
Agfa Ultra	50	135-24/36, 120 roll
Agfa Optima	125	135-24/36, 120 roll
Agfa Optima	200	135-24/36, 120 roll
Agfa Portrait	160	135-24/36, 120 roll
Agfacolor 100	100	135-15/27/36, 120 roll
Agfacolor 200	200	135-15/27/36, 120 roll
Agfacolor 400	400	135-15/27/36, 120 roll
FUJI		
Fujicolor NSP	160	135-36, bulk, 120 roll
Fujicolor Reala	100	135-24/36, 120 roll
Fujicolor Super HG 100	100	135-12/24/36, 120 roll
Fujicolor Super HG 200	200	135-12/24/36
Fujicolor Super HG 400	400	135-12/24/36, 120 roll
Fujicolor Super HG 1600	1600	135-12/24/36
KODAK		
Vericolor III	160	135-24/36, 120 roll
Vericolor 400	400	135-36, 120 roll
Ektacolor 160	160	135-36, 120 roll
Ektar 25	25	135-24/36, 120 roll
Ektar 100	100	135-12/24/36
Ektar 1000	1000	135-24/36
Kodak Gold II	100	135-12/24/36
Kodak Gold II	200	135-12/24/36, 120 roll
Kodak Gold II	400	135-12/24/36
Ektapress 100	100	135-36
Ektapress 400	400	135-36
Ektapress 1600	600	135-36
KONICA		
Color SRG160	160	135-12/24/36, 120 roll
Color Impresa 50	50	135-12/24/36
Color Super SR100	100	135-12/24/36, 120 roll
Color Super SR200	200	135-12/24/36
Color Super SR400	400	135-12/24/36
Color Super SR3200	3200	135-24/36, 120 roll
SCOTCH 3M		
Scotch AT 100	100	135-12/24/36
Scotch AT 200	200	135-24/36
Scotch AT 400	400	135-24/36

Popular colour slide films

Colour slide, or reversal, film requires much more careful exposure than does either black and white or colour negative film, as there is no printing stage where highlights can be burnt in or shadows held back. Modern reversal emulsions do allow a little latitude in exposure – perhaps ½ to 1 *f* stop either side of the correct exposure – but when using slide film it is usually advisable to take a light reading from a highlight and allow the shadows to go a little dark. Underexposing by about ½ a stop should produce good saturated colours.

Name	ISO speed	Sizes generally available
AGFA-GEVAERT		
Agfachrome CT100	100	135-27/36, 120 roll
Agfachrome CT200	200	135-27/36, 120 roll
Agfachrome RS50	50	135-36, 120 roll
Agfachrome RS1000	1000	135-36, 120 roll
FUJI		
Fujichrome Velvia	50	135-36, 120 roll
Fujichrome 50	50	135-24/36, 120 roll
Fujichrome 100	100	135-24/36, 120 roll
Fujichrome 400	400	135-24/36, 120 roll
Fujichrome P1600	1600	135-36
Fujichrome 64T	64	135-36, 120 roll
KODAK		
Kodachrome 25	25	135-24/36
Kodachrome 64	64	135-24/36, 120 roll
Kodachrome 200	200	135-36
Ektachrome 50	50	135-36
Ektachrome 64	64	135-36, 120 roll
Ektachrome 64 X	64	135-36, 120 roll
Ektachrome 100 Plus	100	135-36, 120 roll
Ektachrome 100 HC	100	135-24/36, 120 roll
Ektachrome 100 X	100	135-36, 120 roll
Ektachrome 200	200	135-36, 120 roll
Ektachrome 400	400	135-24/36, 120 roll
Ektachrome 800/1600	1600	135-36
Ektachrome 64T	64	135-36, 120 roll
Ektachrome 160T	160	135-36, 120 roll
Ektachrome SE 50-366	n/a	135-36
Ektachrome Infrared 5	n/a	135-36
Kodak Photomicrography	n/a	135/36
SCOTCH 3M		
Scotch HR 100	100	135-36
Scotch HR 400	400	135-36
Scotch HR 1000	1000	135-36
Scotch HR 640T	640	135-36
Scotch P800/3200	3200	135-36

Popular black and white reversal films

The process of reversing a black and white negative film to produce slides tends to result in weak blacks and muddy whites, so it is best to buy a black and white reversal film.

AGFA-GEVAERT		
Agfa Dia-Direct	32	135-36

Popular instant picture films

Instant picture film is a boon for both the casual photographer and the professional. Any error in exposure, composition or lighting can be seen immediately and another picture taken.

Name	ISO speed	Image	Format
POLAROID			
Type 664	100	b&w print	8.25 x 10.75cm
			(3.25 x 4.25in)
Type 665	50-75	b&w print	8.25 x 10.75cm
Type 667	3000	b&w print	8.25 x 10.75cm
Type 669	80	col print	8.25 x 10.75cm
PC 100	100	col print	8.25 x 10.75cm
Polachrome CS	40	col slide	135-12/36
Polachrome HCP	40	col slide	135-12

Common colour kits for home processing

For colour slide films:	Agfachrome AP44 Kodak E6 Photocolor Chrome 6
For colour negative films (all C-41 compatible):	Agfa AP70 Kodak Flexicolor Paterson 2NA Photocolor FP
For colour prints from negatives:	Agfa AP92 Kodak Ektaprint 2 Photocolor RT Printmaker
For colour prints from slides:	Ilfochrome A (previously known as Cibachrome A) Kodak Ektachrome R-3000 Photocolor Chrome "R"

Chemical functions

First developer	converts the exposed silver halides (latent image) into black metallic silver
Stop bath	a solution used to stop development
Colour developer	converts exposed silver halides to black metallic silver; also produces dye "cloud" around each crystal
Conditioner	prepares metallic silver for bleaching
Bleach and fix	converts metallic silver to a halide similar to the thiosulphate solutions used in black and white processes; reduces silver halides to water-soluble salts
Stabilizer	mild acid used to harden the emulsion

Filters for colour photography

Filters designed specifically for colour photography generally provide very slight colour changes. Correction filters, though, allow film balanced for daylight to be exposed by artificial light, or artificial light film to be exposed by daylight sources.

Even when the type of film in your camera matches the light source used to illuminate the subject, a change in the quality of light may be desired. Often, pictures taken by the sea, or some other large expanse of water, exhibit dull, washed-out colours, and an overall colour cast towards blue. This is usually caused by an excess of ultraviolet light in the atmosphere and can be corrected by using a UV filter over the camera lens. A skylight filter has much the same effect, but its very slight orange colour adds a little warmth to shadow areas and is very useful for making pictures taken on an overcast day appear quite sunny. Polarizing filters, although expensive, are invaluable for darkening a light blue sky and strengthening the contrast between sky and clouds.

Remember that nearly all filters, with the exception of the UV and skylight filters, reduce the amount of light reaching the film and will cause underexposure unless allowed for. To compensate, additional exposure must be given. TTL metering cameras should automatically compensate for any light loss, but non-TTL cameras must be adjusted by referring to the filter factor found on the filter mount (see p.132).

Filters for colour photography	
Filter	Use
Wratten 80B (correction/conversion)	Adds the blue component in photoflood light, raising its colour temperature to almost that of daylight, allowing daylight film to be used indoors with photoflood light.
Wratten 85B (correction/conversion)	Alters the colour temperature of daylight so that artificial light film may be exposed outdoors by daylight or indoors with electronic flash or blue flash bulbs.
FL-D	Converts fluorescent light more closely to the colour temperature of daylight. This allows photography with daylight film indoors by fluorescent light.
UV (ultraviolet) or Skylight (1A)	Reduces UV rays, which would give prints or slides a slight overall blue cast, from reaching the film. This is noticeable on skin tones taken in shady areas under a blue sky. Can be left permanently on the lens for protection against dirt or scratching. Will penetrate the haze that would otherwise partially obscure a distant part of a scene.
Polarizing	Reduces glare and reflections from shiny surfaces (glass, water or polished wood—but *not* metal). The only filter which will darken a light blue sky (not make a grey sky blue) without much affecting other colours.

Contrast filters for black and white film

A contrast filter will effectively lighten the tone of objects the same colour as the filter and render complementary colours as darker toned. As a black and white film may "see" the tones of a red letter box against a green hedge as being nearly the same, the letter box might be difficult to distinguish on a print against the background hedge. By using a green filter the foliage will appear lighter and the red letter box will, by comparison, appear darker. Conversely, a red contrast filter would effectively lighten the red letter box and darken the green background.

As a light reading taken from the sky might indicate an exposure two or three stops less than that indicated by an object at ground level, pretty or dramatic cloud effects have the annoying habit of burning out unless the contrast between clouds and sky is increased (when the picture is taken) by using a yellow, orange or red filter with black and white film or a polarizing filter with colour film. A yellow filter increases contrast a little; a red filter can make fluffy white clouds look like a dark and stormy sky. The darker the sky colour, the more the clouds become noticeable in the photograph.

Filter colour	Tones of colour rendered lighter (by comparison)	Tones of colour rendered darker (by comparison)
Blue	Blue	Yellow Orange Red
Green	Green	Blue Orange Red
Yellow	Yellow Orange Red	Blue
Orange	Orange Red	Blue Green
Red	Red	Blue Green

Filters for colour or black and white film

As nearly all filters prevent some light from reaching the film, an exposure allowance has to be made to prevent underexposure. The filter factor is the number of f-stops the lens needs to be opened to compensate for the light lost.

Filter Type	Colour or Description	Filter Factor	
		Daylight	Tungsten
1A	Skylight	0	0
UV-Haze	Clear	0	0
ND-3	2 × Neutral Density	1	1
ND-6	4 × Neutral Density	2	2

Filters for special effects

Most special-effects filters can be used with black and white, colour negative or colour reversal film. No set guidelines can be laid down for their use, so experimentation is the keyword to success. Although there are quite a number of these filters available, their use should be limited to suitable subjects. Used with discretion they can add sparkle to an otherwise prosaic scene, but the danger always is that the pictorial content of the photograph may become lost. Some filters are available in both glass and gelatin, but the glass filters, although more expensive, are more resistant to abrasion and dust. These filters tend to be expensive so it is best to buy only one or two initially and learn their effects before buying others.

Filter	Use
Graduated colour	Three types available—one colour only, graduated from light to dark: one colour graduating into another colour; one colour which darkens overall by rotating the front of the filter.
Dual colour	A two-coloured piece of glass in a filter mount.
Neutral density	A grey filter used merely to reduce the intensity of the light.
Soft focus	To give the whole picture a slightly fuzzy look.
Soft spot	To give the whole picture—except the subject in the middle of the frame—a slightly fuzzy look.
Close-up	Available in various diopter strengths (+1, +2, +3, +4) to allow a lens to focus on objects closer than it normally could.
Cross-screen or starburst	Used to spread rays of light emanating from a point source of light within a lens's field of view; usually available for four, six or eight points.
Split field	Effectively only half of a close-up lens; this allows distant and close-up subjects to be simultaneously in sharp focus beyond the depth of field associated with a particular lens at a given aperture.
Fog	Gives the picture an overall slight hazy or foggy appearance.
Prism	Available in many types, which can multiply the main subject image three, four, five or six times; for example, three parallel similar images of the subject or one main image surrounded by three or four repeated images of the subject.
Rainbow	Used to diffract light, producing a spectral pattern from any visible point source of light within the scene. The filter mount can be rotated allowing the filter effect to be positioned at any point around the light source.

Daylight exposure guide

Film speed (ISO)	Sunny	Partly cloudy/ Hazy sun	Hazy/bright (indistinct shadows)	Dull (no shadows)
		(+1)	(+2)	(+1)
25	1/30, f16 1/60, f11 1/125, f8	1/30, f11 1/60, f8 1/125, f5.6	1/30, f5.6 1/60, f4 1/125, f2.8	1/30, f4 1/60, f2.8 1/125, f2
50-64	1/60, f16 1/125, f11 1/250, f8	1/60, f11 1/125, f8 1/250, f5.6	1/60, f5.6 1/125, f4 1/250, f2.8	1/60, f4 1/125, f2.8 1/250, f2
80	1/60, f16-f22 1/125, f11-f16 1/250, f8-f11	1/60, f11-f16 1/125, f8-f11 1/250, f5.6-f8	1/60, f5.6-f8 1/125, f4-f5.6 1/250, f2.8-f4	1/60, f4-f5.6 1/125, f2.8-f4 1/250, f2-f2.8
100-125	1/125, f16 1/250, f11 1/500, f8	1/125, f11 1/250, f8 1/500, f5.6	1/125, f5.6 1/250, f4 1/500, f2.8	1/125, f4 1/250, f2.8 1/500, f2
160	1/125, f16-f22 1/250, f11-f16 1/500, f8-f11	1/125, f11-f16 1/250, f8-f11 1/500, f5.6-f8	1/125, f5.6-f8 1/250, f4-f5.6 1/500, f2.8-f4	1/125, f4-f5.6 1/250, f2.8-f4 1/500, f2-f2.8
200	1/125, f16 1/250, f11 1/500, f8	1/250, f11 1/500, f8 1/1000, f5.6	1/250, f5.6 1/500, f4 1/1000, f2.8	1/250, f4 1/500, f2.8 1/1000, f2
400	1/250, f22 1/500, f16 1/1000, f11	1/250, f16 1/500, f11 1/1000, f8	1/250, f8 1/500, f5.6 1/1000, f4	1/250, f5.6 1/500, f4 1/1000, f2.8

A subject in bright, reflective surroundings (on snow, on a beach) should be given the equivalent of one f stop less exposure (the next faster shutter speed or the next smaller f stop) due to the extra light that the surroundings reflect back on to the subject. Similarly, dark subjects in dark surroundings can be given the equivalent of one or two f stops more exposure. These exposures should be taken as a guide only. Due to the capability of the human eye to adjust readily to a decrease or increase in light intensity, the photographer can easily be fooled about exposures. When shooting negative films, it is better to err by overexposing rather than underexposing, as detail can always be "burnt-in" at the printing stage. Exposure on slide films is more critical—once exposed and developed there is precious little that can be done in the way of correcting any error. This is when an exposure meter (built into the camera or a separate hand-held one) is invaluable.

The general guide to an exposure in bright sun is to shoot at f16 at the shutter speed which is the reciprocal of the film speed (in ISO), i.e. with 125 ISO film, use f16 at 1/125 (or any equivalent exposure); with 400 ISO film, use f16 at 1/500 (or equivalent).

When talking about equivalent exposure, it is worth remembering that each full f stop increase (e.g. f11 to f8) represents a doubling of the size of the aperture, allowing twice as much light to reach the film. Moving the shutter speed dial from 1/125 to 1/250, for example, halves the length of time the light is allowed to enter the camera. From this it can be seen that f11, 1/125 is equivalent to f8, 1/250 in terms of the amount of light reaching the film.

Night exposure guide (at 100 ISO)

Subject	f stop/shutter speeds			
	f4	f5.6	f8	f11
Bonfire/fireworks	1/15	1/8	1/4	1/2
Well-lit shop windows	1/30	1/15	1/8	1/4
Well-lit streets	1/4	1/2	1	2
Flood-lit monuments	1	2	4	8
Full-moon landscape	1 min	2 min	4 min	8 min
Well-lit store interiors	1/15	1/8	1/4	1/2
Well-lit stage	1/30	1/15	1/8	1/4
Average home lighting (close to subject)	1/4	1/2	1	2

Shoot night scenes, if possible, before the sky goes completely black. Dusk is best, as there is still enough available light to fill in detail and provide some modelling; the above exposure times may then be halved. Remember that many such "night" scenes will not benefit from the relatively small amount of light from an ordinary amateur flashgun. Bonfire and fireworks pictures, for example, *cannot* be taken with flash as the flash will kill the atmosphere and effects you are trying to capture on film. The resulting long exposures require the use of a tripod or other camera-steadying device and a cable release to avoid camera shake and blurred pictures.

Stage performers and sportsmen do not welcome flash being used during their performances. In many cases flash will not ensure a good exposure anyway and will annoy the performer and audience. It is often prohibited, so always check with the organizers first.

By using a wider lens aperture and a faster film (e.g. 400 ISO) you can sometimes reduce exposure time so that you do not need a tripod and cable release. These exposures should be taken only as a guide. Bracketing will probably be necessary to ensure a good exposure; take a second picture, giving it half the recommended exposure and a third giving it twice the exposure.

If, during an exposure of longer than about 4 sec, a moving subject (pedestrian, car, etc.) travels across the picture area, simply cover the lens with your hand or a piece of card until the interference has passed; then remove the cover to continue the remainder of the exposure, adding on the time the lens was covered.

With exposures longer than about 1 sec, the reciprocity factor should be considered. This means that in a given situation, closing the lens aperture by one stop does not necessarily call for twice the exposure time, but probably a bit more. It is safer to add a few extra seconds exposure time for shots which call for several seconds initially, and to bracket exposure around this assumed exposure time if possible. The reciprocity factor will also affect the colour balance of colour film.

Working with black and white film also allows you the option of uprating, or pushing, your film. For example, 400 ISO film can be exposed as if it were 800 ISO. Adjustments can be made at the development stage to compensate for this one-stop underexposure, and acceptable, if grainy, pictures will result.

Colour temperature and filtration

Light source	Colour temperature Kelvins	Filtration with daylight balanced film	Filtration with tungsten balanced film
Blue sky	20,000	85B	
	15,000		
		85	
	10,000	85C	
Hazy sunlight	9,000		
Average in shade, summer	8,000		
		81EF	
Overcast sky	7,000	81C	
Lightly overcast sky	6,500	81B	
	6,000	81A	
		81	
Summer sunlight	5,500	No filter	85B
	5,000	82	
		82A	85
Early morning and late afternoon sunlight	4,500	82B 82C	85C
		80D	
	4,000		
		80C	81EF 81C
1hr after sunrise/ before sunset	3,500		81B
Photoflood bulb	3,400	80B	81A
	3,300		81
Tungsten halogen lamp	3,200	80A	No filter
	3,100		82
	3,000		82A
100 watt light bulb	2,900		82B
	2,800		82C
40 watt light bulb	2,700		80D

From elementary physics we know that "white" light is made up of all the colours in the spectrum. Photographically, a film sees daylight with a bluish tinge and artificial tungsten light with a yellowish tinge. This is why two types of colour film are available—one for daylight (or electronic flash or blue flash bulbs) and another for artificial or tungsten light sources (or clear flash bulbs). They are said to be balanced for daylight or artificial light (Type B film) which relates to faithfully reproducing colours seen in bluish or yellowish light. Human eyes can adjust to this slight colour change—film (on its own, unaided by lens filters) cannot.

Each light source, be it a household tungsten light bulb, the sun or a hazy sky, has its own rating, called "colour temperature". The more blue, the higher its colour temperature; the more yellow, the lower its colour temperature. Colour temperature is measured in units of degrees on the Kelvin scale (0°K = −273°C). Colour conversion or correction filters can be used in order to obtain correct colours in a scene taken with artificial light film illuminated by daylight or with daylight film illuminated by artificial light.

Flashgun guide number

A flashgun's guide number is the indication of its lighting power. It is a figure quoted either in feet or metres at a given film speed (usually ISO). For example, a flash unit with a guide number of 16 (m) at 100 ISO is half as strong as a flash unit with a guide

Flashgun guide number (continued)

number of 22 (m) at 100 ISO.

When you change to a film of a different speed, you will need to know the GN of your gun *at the new film speed*. For example if a flashgun has a GN of about 16 (m) using 100 ISO film, it will have a GN of 22 (m) using 200 ISO film. Generally speaking, to calculate the correct lens aperture to use with flash (the shutter speed being determined by the camera manufacturer to synchronize at a particular setting), divide the flash unit's GN by the flash-to-subject distance. For this purpose, both the GN and flash-to-subject distance must be in the same measurement unit, i.e. both feet or both metres.

BCPS (beam candlepower second) output is a rating for the amount of light a particular flashgun puts out. W-S (watt-second) is the amount of energy discharged by the flashgun. One watt-second is approximately equal to 40 lumen-seconds.

	25	50	64	80	100	160	200	BCPS	W-S
				ISO FILM SPEED					
M	6	9	10	11	12	16	18	300	8
F	20	28	32	35	40	50	56		
M	7	10	11	12	14	18	20	375	10
F	22	32	35	40	45	56	63		
M	8	11	12	14	16	20	22	450	12
F	25	35	40	45	50	63	70		
M	9	12	14	16	18	22	25	600	16
F	28	40	45	50	56	70	80		
M	10	14	16	18	20	25	28	750	20
F	32	45	50	56	63	80	90		
M	11	16	18	20	22	28	32	900	25
F	35	50	56	63	70	90	100		
M	12	18	20	22	25	32	35	1200	32
F	40	56	63	70	80	100	110		
M	14	20	22	25	28	35	40	1500	40
F	45	63	70	80	90	110	125		
M	16	22	25	28	32	40	45	1800	50
F	50	70	80	90	100	125	140		
M	18	25	28	32	35	45	50	2400	64
F	56	80	90	100	110	140	160		
M	20	28	32	35	40	50	56	3000	80
F	63	90	100	110	125	160	180		
M	22	32	35	40	45	56	63	3600	100
F	70	100	110	125	140	180	200		
M	25	35	40	45	50	63	70	4800	125
F	80	110	125	140	160	200	220		
M	28	40	45	50	56	70	80	6000	160
F	90	125	140	160	180	220	250		
M	32	45	50	56	63	80	90	7200	200
F	100	140	160	180	200	250	280		

Glossary

Achromatic lens Lens design using two pieces of different glass to bring two different colours of the spectrum to a common point of focus.

Aerial perspective Noticed as the result of dust and moisture particles in the atmosphere, scattering light of a short wavelength (blue light) most. Gives the impression of various tones of blue in distant landscapes.

Aperture Size of the lens diaphragm opening through which light enters the camera to reach the film.

Barn doors Side flaps surrounding a spotlight. Used to concentrate the spread of light.

Bellows Adjustable sleeve between camera body and lens. Provides the extension between body and lens necessary for taking close-ups.

Bounce flash Flash reflected from any surface before it reaches the subject. Gives a soft, even light.

Bracketing Taking additional photographs at twice and half the recommended exposure to ensure correct exposure.

Cable release Device that screws into the shutter release allowing the shutter to be triggered from a distance. A cable release minimizes camera shake.

Camera movements Altering the relative planes of the lens panel and camera back, and moving the lens at right angles to its axis. These features normally only found on large-format cameras, except for the rise and fall facility of the 35 mm format shift lens.

Cartridge Plastic holder for 126 and 110 film.

Cassette Light-tight container used for 35 mm film.

CdS (cadmium sulphide) Light-sensitive cell used in exposure meters. Batteries are needed.

Chromatic aberration The inability of a lens to bring light of all colours to a common point of focus.

Colour temperature The measurement of light source in terms of colour quality. Expressed in degrees Kelvin.

Converging verticals Noticed when the camera lens is pointed away from a parallel position. Verticals appear to meet in the distance.

Cropping Altering the image by omitting certain elements. Used either at the picture-taking stage or printing stage.

Depth of field The area surrounding the true point of focus where the image still appears acceptably sharp.

Diaphragm The adjustable aperture blades of a lens; sometimes called iris.

Dichroic filters Dial-in filters found in colour heads of some enlargers. Used instead of separate square filter gels.

Double exposure Exposing the same piece of film or light-sensitive paper twice.

Drying marks Stains left on films or prints when water from the surface evaporates. Wetting agent used in the final rinse to reduce the surface tension of water, so promoting even drying.

Dye coupler Chemical that reacts with oxidized developer to form a colour image.

Electronic flash Compact source of artificial light. Gives a relatively high power output of the same quality as daylight. Can be attached to the camera's hot shoe or accessory shoe or connected by a sync lead.

Exposure The amount of light allowed to reach a light-sensitive material.

Exposure meter (or light meter) Device for measuring the amount of light falling on, or refelected from, an object.

Extension tubes Tubes that fit between the camera body and lens. Provide fixed ratios of subject enlargement for close-ups.

Film speed A numerical expression of a film's sensitivity to light, measured in either ASA or ISO.

Filter Disc (usually glass) that fits over the camera lens and absorbs certain parts of incident light and transmits the rest.

Filter factor The amount by which exposure has to be adjusted to compensate for the light-blocking power of a filter.

Flash umbrella Reflective umbrella used to bounce light from a flash or other light source on to the subject.

F-number (or f-stop) Numerical expression of the size of the aperture at its different settings.

Focal plane The plane where light entering the lens forms a sharp image.

Focal plane shutter Shutter system situated as near the focal plane as possible.

Focus magnifier Device that magnifies the grain of a negative, as projected by an enlarger, allowing a sharply focused image to be seen.

Focusing screen Etched glass screen incorporated in the camera on which the image is focused by moving the lens.

F-stop See f-number.

Glass-beaded screen Projection screen covered with glass beads to give a narrow angle of reflection and a very bright image.

Grain Visual impression of clumps of silver or their associated dye images.

Guide number Numerical expression of a flashgun's lighting intensity. The number divided by the flash-to-subject distance gives the aperture needed for correct exposure.

Halogen Generic name for group of elements containing iodine, chlorine, bromine and fluorine. These, used in compounds with a metal, are called halides.

High key Photograph containing mostly light tones.

Highlight Bright area of a subject. Reproduces as a dense part of a negative and prints as a bright area.

Hot shoe Electrical contact for flash synchronization, usually found on top of a camera.

Infra-red Part of the invisible spectrum with a wavelength longer than that of visible red light.

Iris diaphragm Aperture mechanism with adjustable metal leaves.

IR setting Infra-red focus setting found on some lenses. Differs from normal focus as infra-red light focuses farther from the lens.

ISO (International Standards Organization) A numerical rating of a film's sensitivity to light. A high ISO number denotes a fast film – one that is highly sensitive to light, and thus suitable for use in poor lighting conditions.

Kelvin Unit of temperature measurement starting at −273°C (absolute zero). Used to measure the colour quality of light.

Glossary

Latent image Invisible image formed by the action of light on photographic emulsion before development.

Lens hood Metal or rubber shield designed to stop non-image-forming light reaching the lens.

Long lens Lens with a focal length longer than the diagonal of the negative it covers. See also Telephoto lens.

Low key Photograph containing a majority of dark tones.

Macro lens Lens designed for close focusing, giving an image size up to life-size.

Microprisms Minute prisms moulded to the focusing screen to assist focusing the image.

Mirror lens Lens type which uses mirrors in addition to glass elements to provide a physically short lens with a long focal length.

Motor drive Electric motor that automatically winds on the film and retensions the shutter between frames. Takes up to 5 frames per second.

Negative Image where light tones are rendered as dark and dark tones as light, or where colours appear as their complementaries.

Optical axis Imaginary line running through the centre of an optical system at a right angle to the image and film planes.

Orthochromatic Describes emulsions that are insensitive to light of the red wavelength. These can be handled under safelight conditions for short periods without fogging.

Panchromatic Describes materials that are sensitive to light of all colours, but not uniformly so.

Panning Moving the camera to follow a subject during the exposure.

Parallax error Error caused by the slightly different angle of view of the taking lens and the viewing lens.

Photoflood High-output photographic lamp with a short life. Very common form of supplementary lighting.

Pinhole camera Simple camera utilizing a tiny hole instead of a lens. Gives an indistinct image.

Plate camera Large-format camera using either photographic plates or cut film.

Rangefinder Optical distance measuring device usually coupled to the focusing mechanism of the camera.

Ready light Neon lamp on flashguns indicating when batteries have recycled and are ready to fire again.

Reciprocity law Law that states exposure is equal to the intensity of light multiplied by its duration. In very brief or very long exposures this law fails to operate, and you need additional exposure. Colour balance may also be affected.

Reversing ring Adaptor allowing the camera lens to be mounted back to front for close focusing; aperture must then be manually stopped down.

Ring flash Circular flash attachment that fits round the front of the lens. Used to produce shadowless photographs of close-up subjects.

Safelight A dim light source by which certain films and printing paper can be safely handled without damage by fogging.

Selective focusing (also known as differential focusing) Method of utilizing depth of field to render only a small part of the image acceptably sharp.

Selenium cell Light-sensitive cell used in exposure meters. Does not need batteries.

Shift lens (also known as perspective control lens) Wide-angle lens for 35 mm format, which can be moved off its normal axis to provide control over perspective—especially converging verticals.

Shutter Device (usually mechanical) used to control the length of time film is exposed to light.

Shutter speed The length of time a shutter stays open.

Silica-gel Moisture-absorbing crystals used to keep cameras and photographic materials dry. Can be dried out and reused.

Silicon cell Light-sensitive cell used in some fast-reacting TTL light meters. Requires battery power.

Slave unit Photo-electric device used to fire a flash unit when activated by the light from the main flash. Needs no connecting cables.

Snoot Tubular attachment for photographic lamps used to concentrate a beam of light.

Soft-focus lens Any lens incapable of pin-point definition. Filters are available to make an image less critically sharp intentionally.

Spectrum Colours in the visible part of the electro-magnetic radiation produced by dispersion or diffraction. The colours are divided into red, orange, yellow, green, blue, indigo and violet.

Spotlight Lamp utilizing a reflector and movable lens to control the spread of light.

Spot meter Reflected light exposure meter with a very small angle of acceptance.

Standard lens Lens with a focal length approximately equal to the diagonal of the negative it covers. Has an angle of view almost the same as the human eye.

Stopping down Closing the aperture down manually to a preselected *f*-stop.

Sync lead Cable between flashgun and camera body allowing flash to be fired when the shutter is open.

Telephoto converter Auxiliary glass elements, which, when used with the prime lens, magnify a part of the image of the prime lens to simulate a lens of greater focal length.

Telephoto lens Compact lens with a focal length greater than the diagonal of the negative it covers. Used for photographing distant subjects.

Tone Refers to the range of greys between black and white.

Transparency (or slide) A positive image designed to be viewed by transmitted light.

Tungsten lighting Light source with a tungsten filament inside a glass envelope.

Ultraviolet Part of the invisible spectrum with a wavelength shorter than that of blue light. Makes distant scenes appear hazy and causes a blue colour distortion.

Uprating Using a film at a higher speed than the one it was designed for. This effectively underexposes the film and is compensated for by extra development time.

Viewfinder Screen incorporated in a camera or a separate frame that indicates the field of view of a lens.

Wide-angle lens Lens with a focal length shorter than the diagonal of the negative it covers.

X-sync Shutter speed that synchronizes with electronic flash.

Zoom lens Lens type with movable elements allowing the focal length to be varied.

Index

Index